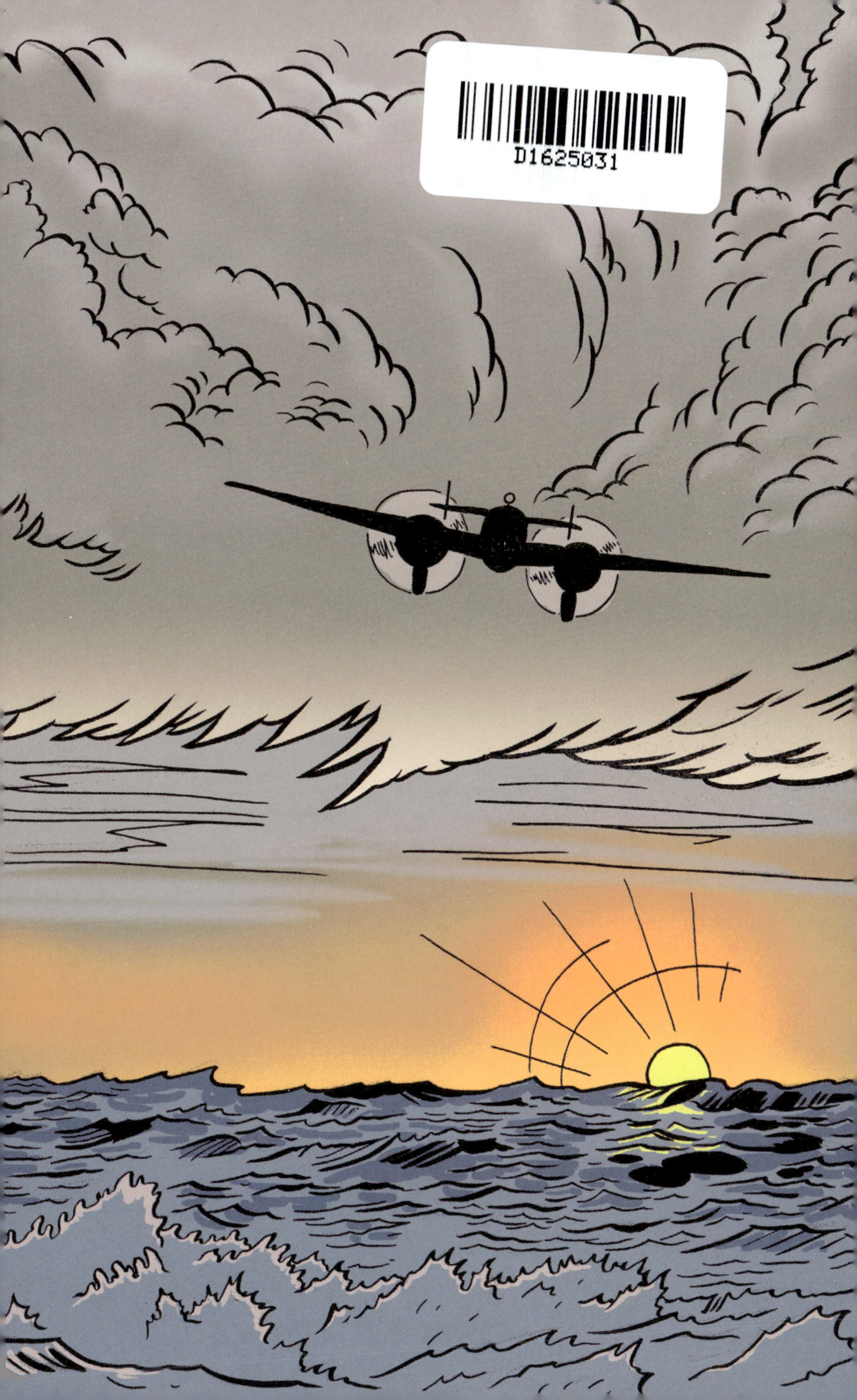

SHOW ME HISTORY!

AMELIA EARHART

PIONEER of the SKY!

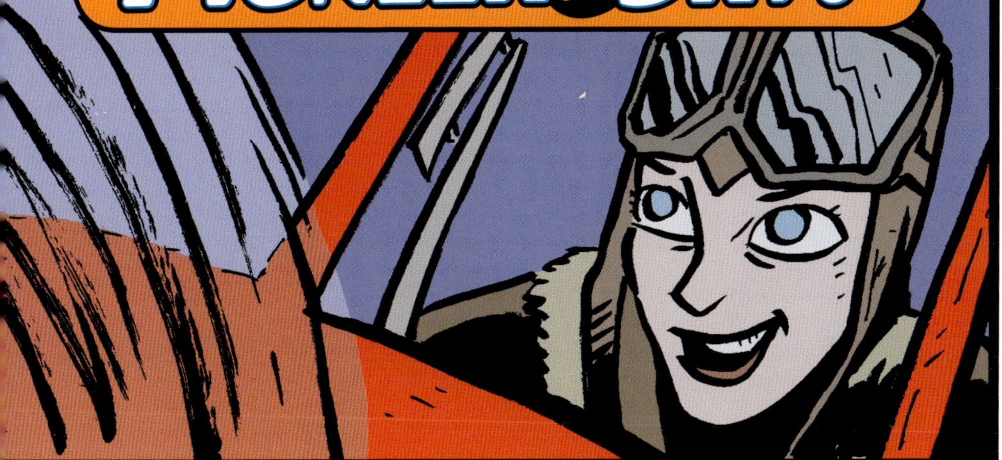

BY

JAMES BUCKLEY JR.

ILLUSTRATED BY

KELLY TINDALL

LETTERING & DESIGN BY

COMICRAFT

COVER ART BY

IAN CHURCHILL

PORTABLE PRESS

SAN DIEGO, CALIFORNIA

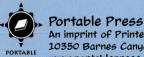

Portable Press

An imprint of Printers Row Publishing Group
10350 Barnes Canyon Road, Suite 100, San Diego, CA 92121
www.portablepress.com • mail@portablepress.com

Printers Row Publishing Group is a division of Readerlink Distribution Services, LLC. Portable Press is a registered trademark of Readerlink Distribution Services, LLC.

Correspondence regarding the content of this book should be addressed to Portable Press, Editorial Department, at the above address. Author and illustration inquiries should be addressed to Oomf, Inc., www.oomf.com.

Publisher: Peter Norton
Associate Publisher: Ana Parker
Developmental Editor: Vicki Jaeger
Publishing Team: Kathryn C. Dalby, Lauren Taniguchi
Production Team: Jonathan Lopes, Rusty von Dyl

Created at Oomf, Inc., www.Oomf.com
Director: Mark Shulman
Producer: James Buckley Jr.

Written by James Buckley Jr.
Illustrated by Kelly Tindall
Lettering & design by Comicraft: John Roshell, Sarah Jacobs, Niklas Pousette Harger
Cover illustration by Ian Churchill

Library of Congress Cataloging-in-Publication Data

Names: Buckley, James, Jr., 1963- author.
Title: Amelia Earhart : pioneer of the sky! / James Buckley, illustrated by Kelly Tindall ; interior lettering by John Roshell.
Description: San Diego, CA : Printers Row Publishing Group, [2019] | Series: Show me history! | Audience: Ages 8-12. | Audience: Grades 4 to 6.
Identifiers: LCCN 2018030622 | ISBN 9781684125456
Subjects: LCSH: Earhart, Amelia, 1897-1937--Juvenile literature. | Earhart, Amelia, 1897-1937--Comic books, strips, etc. | Women air pilots--United States--Biography--Juvenile literature. | Women air pilots--United States--Biography--Comic books, strips, etc. | Air pilots--United States--Biography--Juvenile literature. | Air pilots--United States--Biography--Comic books, strips, etc. | LCGFT: Nonfiction comics. | Graphic novels.
Classification: LCC TL540.E3 B835 2019 | DDC 629.13092--dc23
LC record available at https://lccn.loc.gov/2018030622

Printed in China

23 22 21 20 19   3 4 5 6 7

LOOK! UP IN THE SKY!

IS IT A **BIRD**?

IS IT A **PLANE**?

OR IS IT A **PIONEER IN A PLANE**?!

IT'S **AMELIA EARHART!**

I'M **LIBBY**. YOU MIGHT KNOW ME AS "LADY LIBERTY," THE STATUE THAT STANDS IN NEW YORK CITY'S HARBOR.

I'LL BE ONE OF YOUR GUIDES AS WE **SHOW YOU** HISTORY!

AND I'M **SAM**! I MIGHT NOT **LOOK** OLD ENOUGH, BUT SOON I'LL BE "UNCLE SAM," A LIVING SYMBOL OF THE UNITED STATES.

TOGETHER, WE'LL TAKE YOU ON A **HIGH-FLYING ADVENTURE** TO MEET ONE OF THE MOST **AMAZING WOMEN** OF ALL TIME.

AMELIA GREW UP IN A TIME WHEN WOMEN WERE NOT EXPECTED TO DO ANYTHING DARING OR DANGEROUS.

BUT THINGS WERE CHANGING, AND SHE WAS READY TO LEAD THE WAY.

AIRPLANES WERE STILL PRETTY NEW IN 1921, WHEN SHE TOOK HER FIRST FLYING LESSON. VERY FEW WOMEN WERE PILOTS.

AMELIA'S SKILL AND DARING SHOWED THAT WOMEN COULD BE GREAT PILOTS.

IN FACT, SAM, WOMEN CAN BE GREAT AT **ANYTHING**!

YOU'RE RIGHT, AS USUAL, LIBBY!

We are by**rking** a head and rai**d** Heaviest s**...** l have e**v...** been in.

AS WE GO ALONG, IF YOU SEE A LETTER THAT AMELIA WROTE, THOSE ARE HER **REAL WORDS**...

...AND A **YELLOW BALLOON** HIGHLIGHTS WHAT AMELIA ACTUALLY SAID!

IN AVIATION, THE WOMAN WHO CAN CREATE HER OWN **JOB** IS THE WOMAN WHO WILL WIN FAME AND FORTUNE.

EVERYTHING ELSE IS BASED ON WHAT WE KNOW ABOUT AMELIA'S LIFE.

ENOUGH CHITCHAT. LET'S GET **STARTED**!

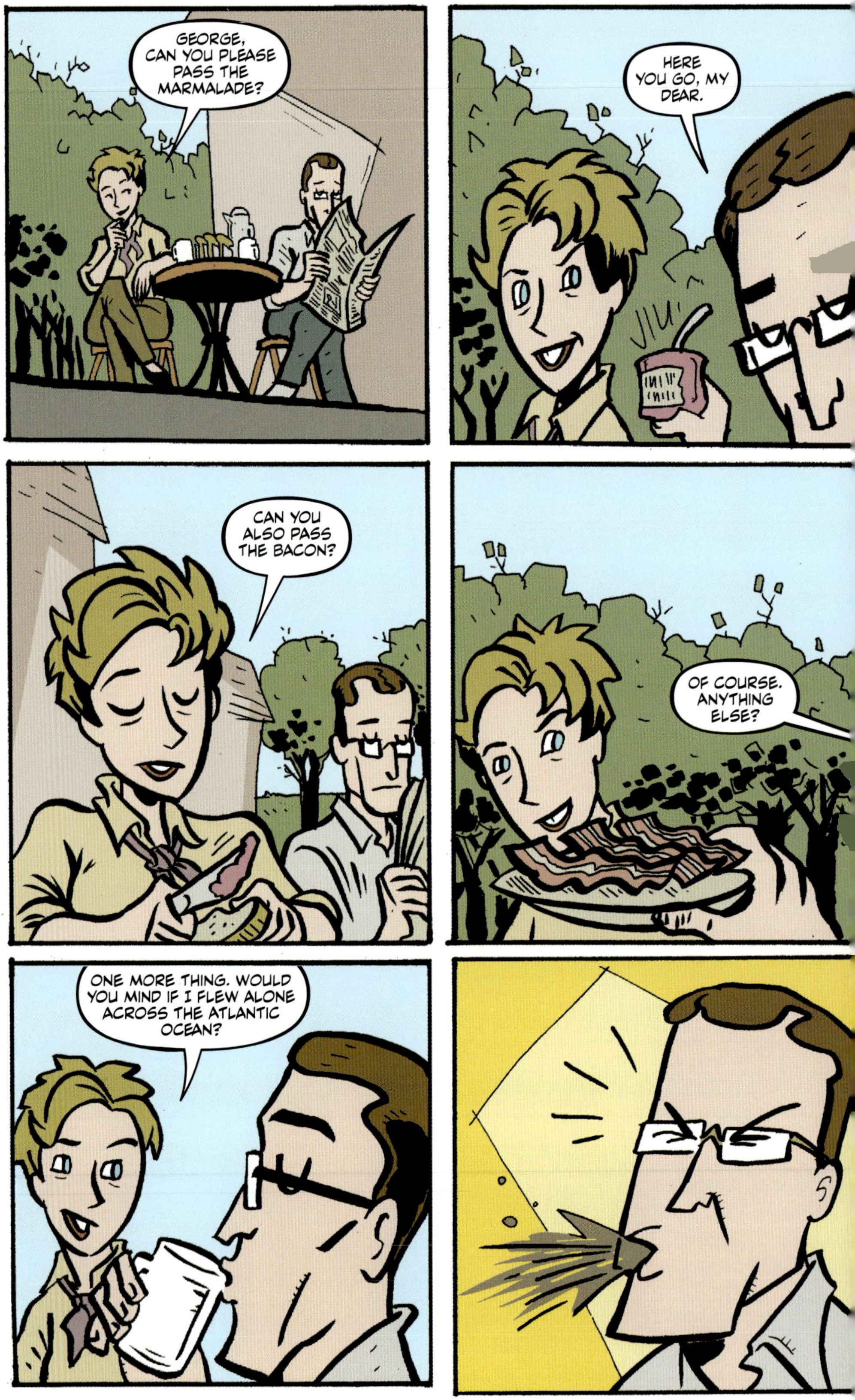
GEORGE, CAN YOU PLEASE PASS THE MARMALADE?
HERE YOU GO, MY DEAR.
CAN YOU ALSO PASS THE BACON?
OF COURSE. ANYTHING ELSE?
ONE MORE THING. WOULD YOU MIND IF I FLEW ALONE ACROSS THE ATLANTIC OCEAN?

1932

HA! NICE GOING, DUDE!

ACTUALLY, GEORGE PUTNAM SHOULD NOT HAVE BEEN THAT SURPRISED. AFTER ALL, HIS WIFE WAS **AMELIA EARHART.**

SO?

SO THIS WAS 1932 AND AMELIA WAS THE MOST **FAMOUS FEMALE FLYER** THE WORLD HAD EVER SEEN.

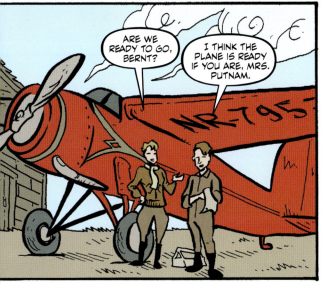

ARE WE READY TO GO, BERNT?

I THINK THE PLANE IS READY IF YOU ARE, MRS. PUTNAM.

THAT'S **MISS EARHART,** PLEASE, BERNT. MR. PUTNAM IS MY HUSBAND, BUT HE DOESN'T OWN ME.

WE WISH YOU THE BEST OF LUCK ON YOUR AMAZING FLIGHT.

THANK YOU, SIR. I HOPE THAT LUCK HAS LITTLE TO DO WITH IT.

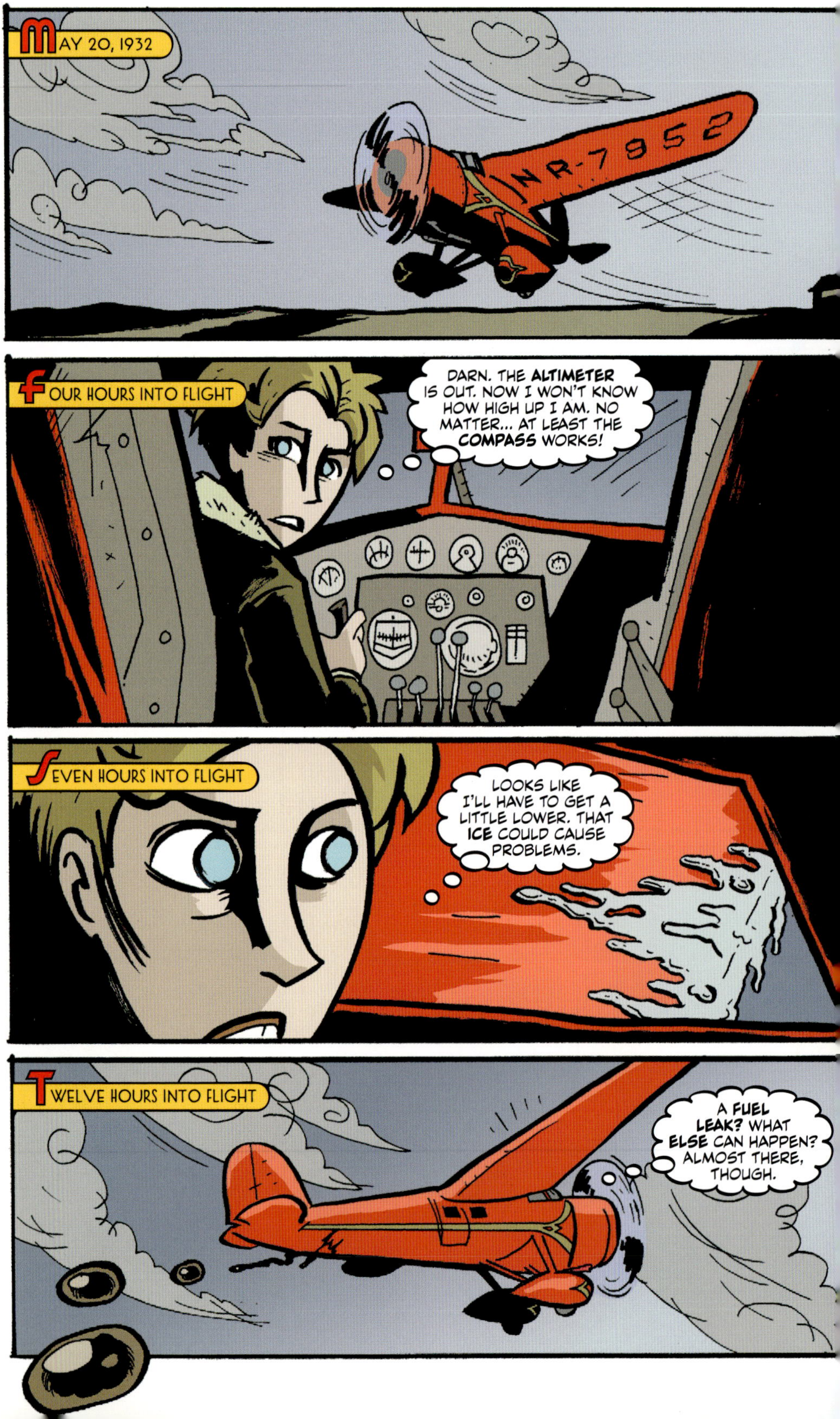
MAY 20, 1932
NR-7952
FOUR HOURS INTO FLIGHT
DARN. THE ALTIMETER IS OUT. NOW I WON'T KNOW HOW HIGH UP I AM. NO MATTER... AT LEAST THE COMPASS WORKS!
SEVEN HOURS INTO FLIGHT
LOOKS LIKE I'LL HAVE TO GET A LITTLE LOWER. THAT ICE COULD CAUSE PROBLEMS.
TWELVE HOURS INTO FLIGHT
A FUEL LEAK? WHAT ELSE CAN HAPPEN? ALMOST THERE, THOUGH.

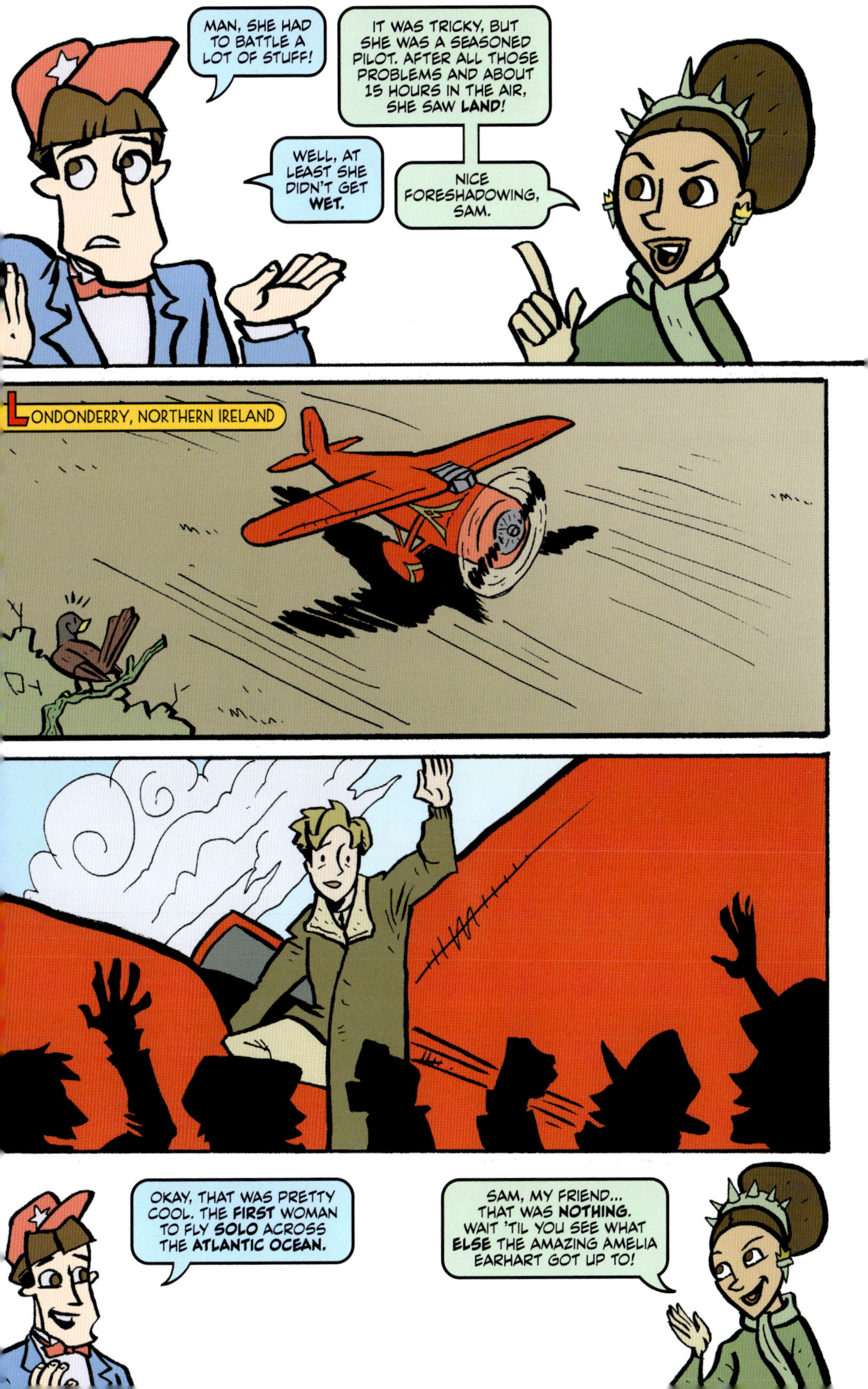
MAN, SHE HAD TO BATTLE A LOT OF STUFF!
IT WAS TRICKY, BUT SHE WAS A SEASONED PILOT. AFTER ALL THOSE PROBLEMS AND ABOUT 15 HOURS IN THE AIR, SHE SAW **LAND**!
WELL, AT LEAST SHE DIDN'T GET **WET.**
NICE FORESHADOWING, SAM.
LONDONDERRY, NORTHERN IRELAND
OKAY, THAT WAS PRETTY COOL. THE **FIRST** WOMAN TO FLY **SOLO** ACROSS THE **ATLANTIC OCEAN.**
SAM, MY FRIEND... THAT WAS **NOTHING**. WAIT 'TIL YOU SEE WHAT **ELSE** THE AMAZING AMELIA EARHART GOT UP TO!

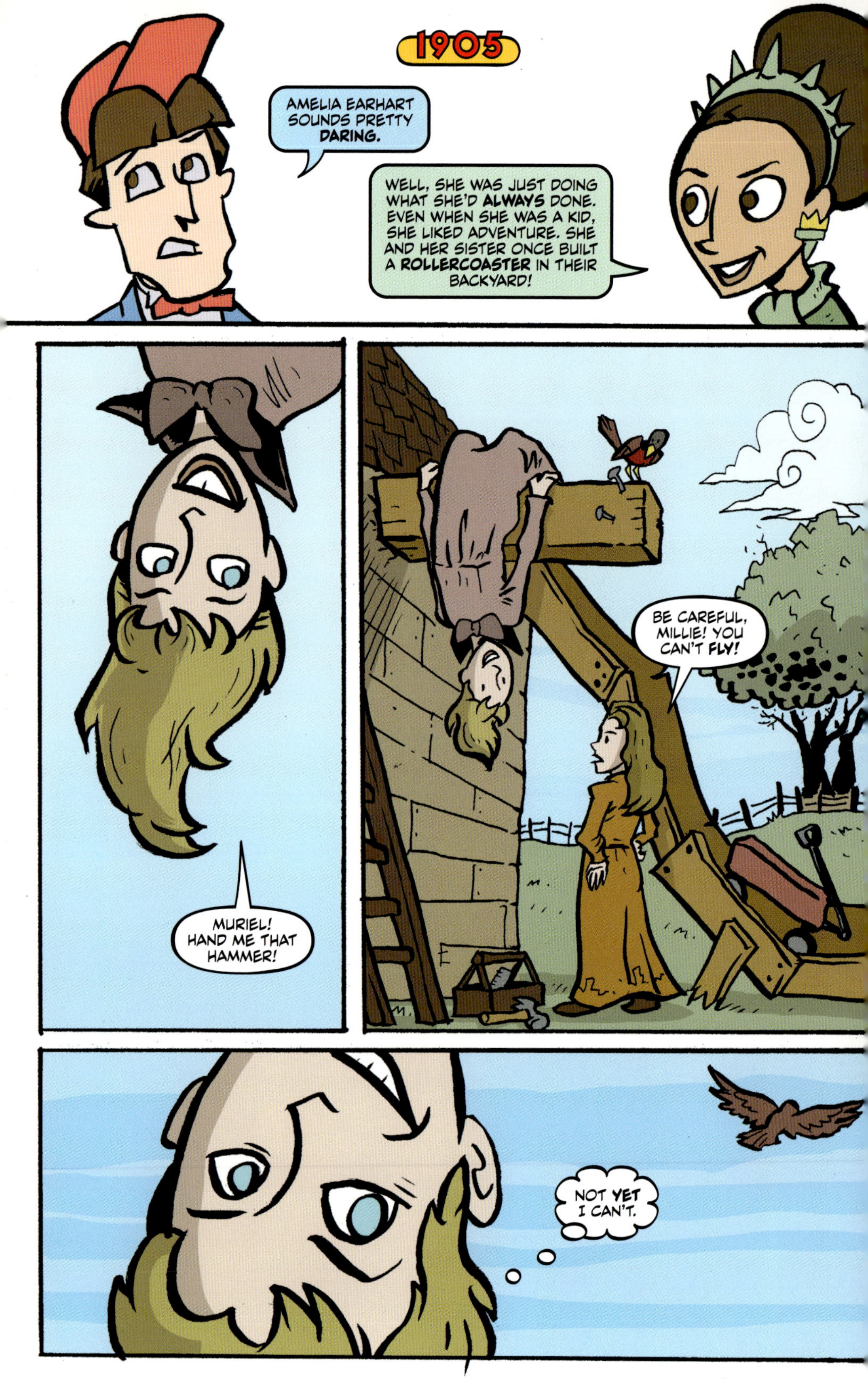
1905
AMELIA EARHART SOUNDS PRETTY DARING.
WELL, SHE WAS JUST DOING WHAT SHE'D ALWAYS DONE. EVEN WHEN SHE WAS A KID, SHE LIKED ADVENTURE. SHE AND HER SISTER ONCE BUILT A ROLLERCOASTER IN THEIR BACKYARD!
MURIEL! HAND ME THAT HAMMER!
BE CAREFUL, MILLIE! YOU CAN'T FLY!
NOT YET I CAN'T.

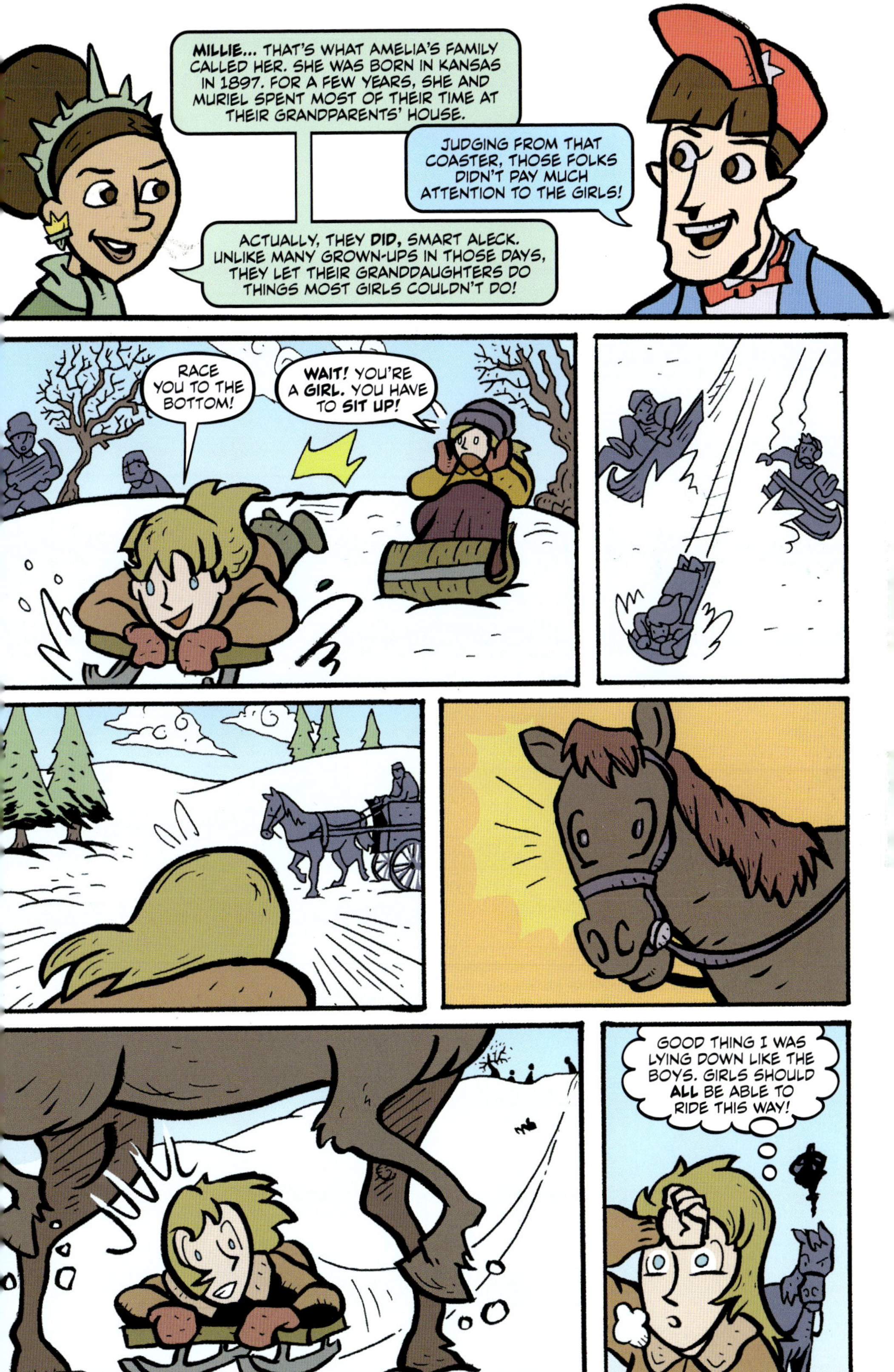
MILLIE... THAT'S WHAT AMELIA'S FAMILY CALLED HER. SHE WAS BORN IN KANSAS IN 1897. FOR A FEW YEARS, SHE AND MURIEL SPENT MOST OF THEIR TIME AT THEIR GRANDPARENTS' HOUSE.
JUDGING FROM THAT COASTER, THOSE FOLKS DIDN'T PAY MUCH ATTENTION TO THE GIRLS!
ACTUALLY, THEY DID, SMART ALECK. UNLIKE MANY GROWN-UPS IN THOSE DAYS, THEY LET THEIR GRANDDAUGHTERS DO THINGS MOST GIRLS COULDN'T DO!
RACE YOU TO THE BOTTOM!
WAIT! YOU'RE A GIRL. YOU HAVE TO SIT UP!
GOOD THING I WAS LYING DOWN LIKE THE BOYS. GIRLS SHOULD ALL BE ABLE TO RIDE THIS WAY!

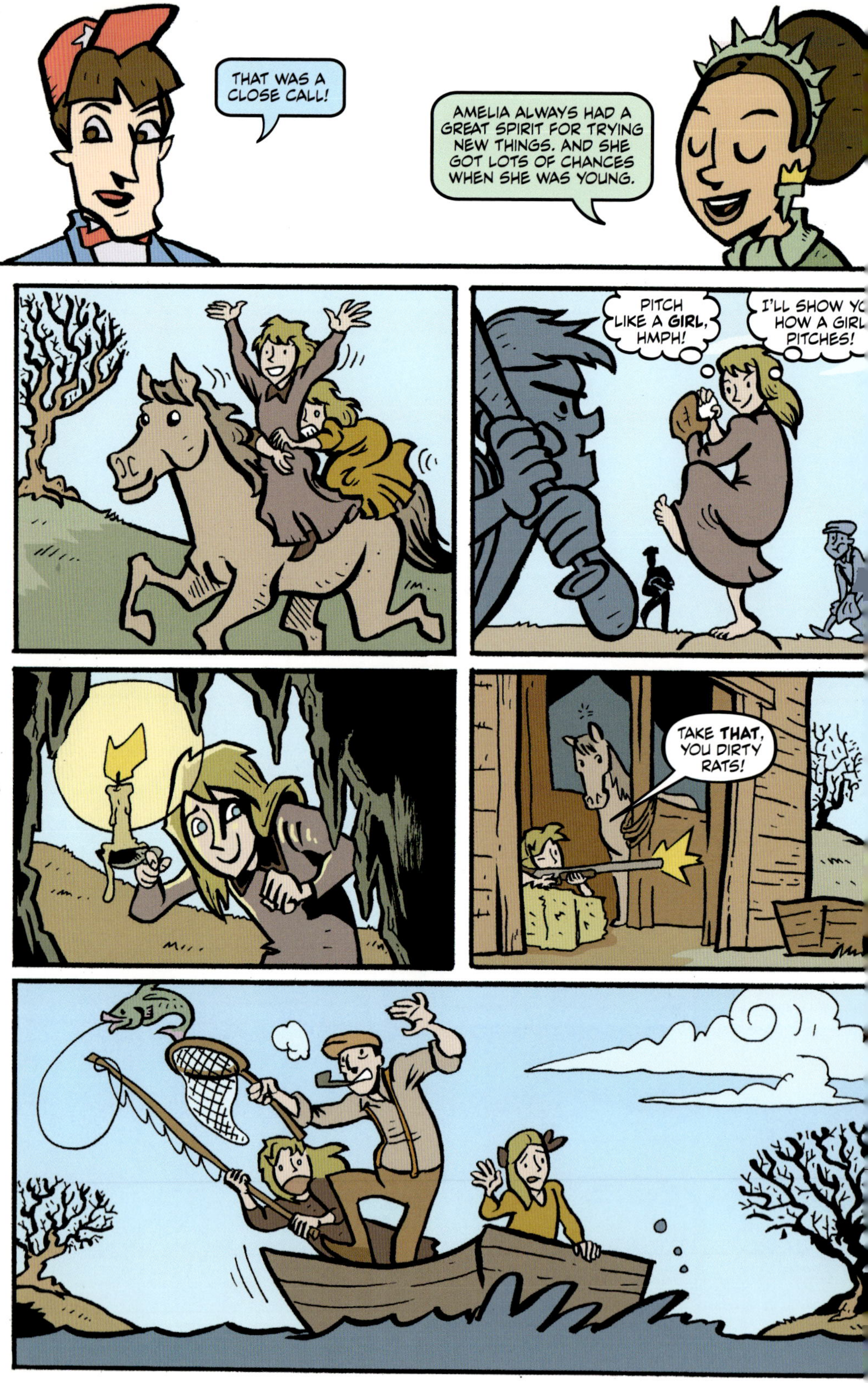

THAT WAS A CLOSE CALL!
AMELIA ALWAYS HAD A GREAT SPIRIT FOR TRYING NEW THINGS. AND SHE GOT LOTS OF CHANCES WHEN SHE WAS YOUNG.
PITCH LIKE A **GIRL**, HMPH!
I'LL SHOW YO HOW A GIRL PITCHES!
TAKE **THAT**, YOU DIRTY RATS!

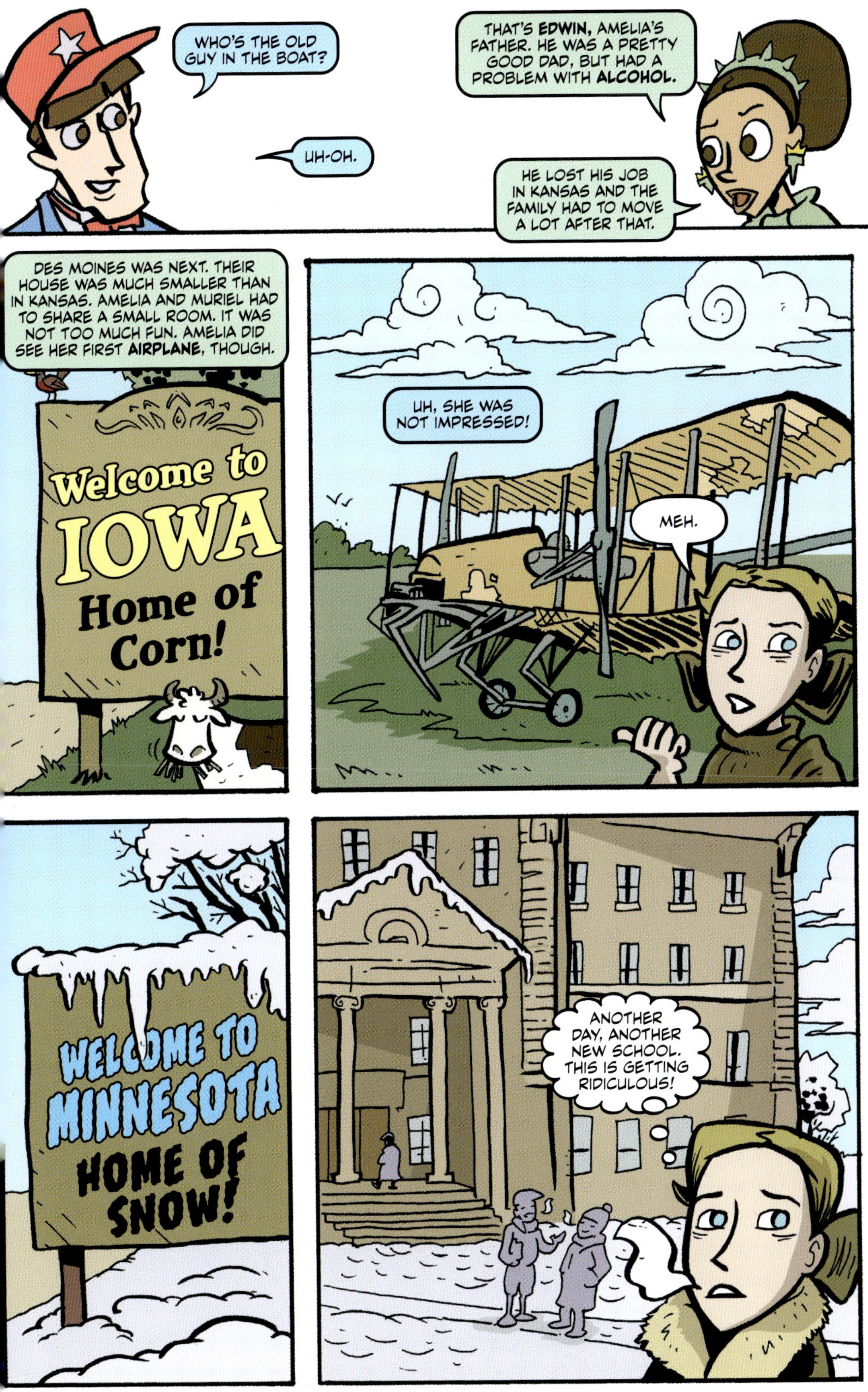
WHO'S THE OLD GUY IN THE BOAT?
UH-OH.
THAT'S EDWIN, AMELIA'S FATHER. HE WAS A PRETTY GOOD DAD, BUT HAD A PROBLEM WITH ALCOHOL.
HE LOST HIS JOB IN KANSAS AND THE FAMILY HAD TO MOVE A LOT AFTER THAT.
DES MOINES WAS NEXT. THEIR HOUSE WAS MUCH SMALLER THAN IN KANSAS. AMELIA AND MURIEL HAD TO SHARE A SMALL ROOM. IT WAS NOT TOO MUCH FUN. AMELIA DID SEE HER FIRST AIRPLANE, THOUGH.
Welcome to IOWA Home of Corn!
UH, SHE WAS NOT IMPRESSED!
MEH.
WELCOME TO MINNESOTA HOME OF SNOW!
ANOTHER DAY, ANOTHER NEW SCHOOL. THIS IS GETTING RIDICULOUS!

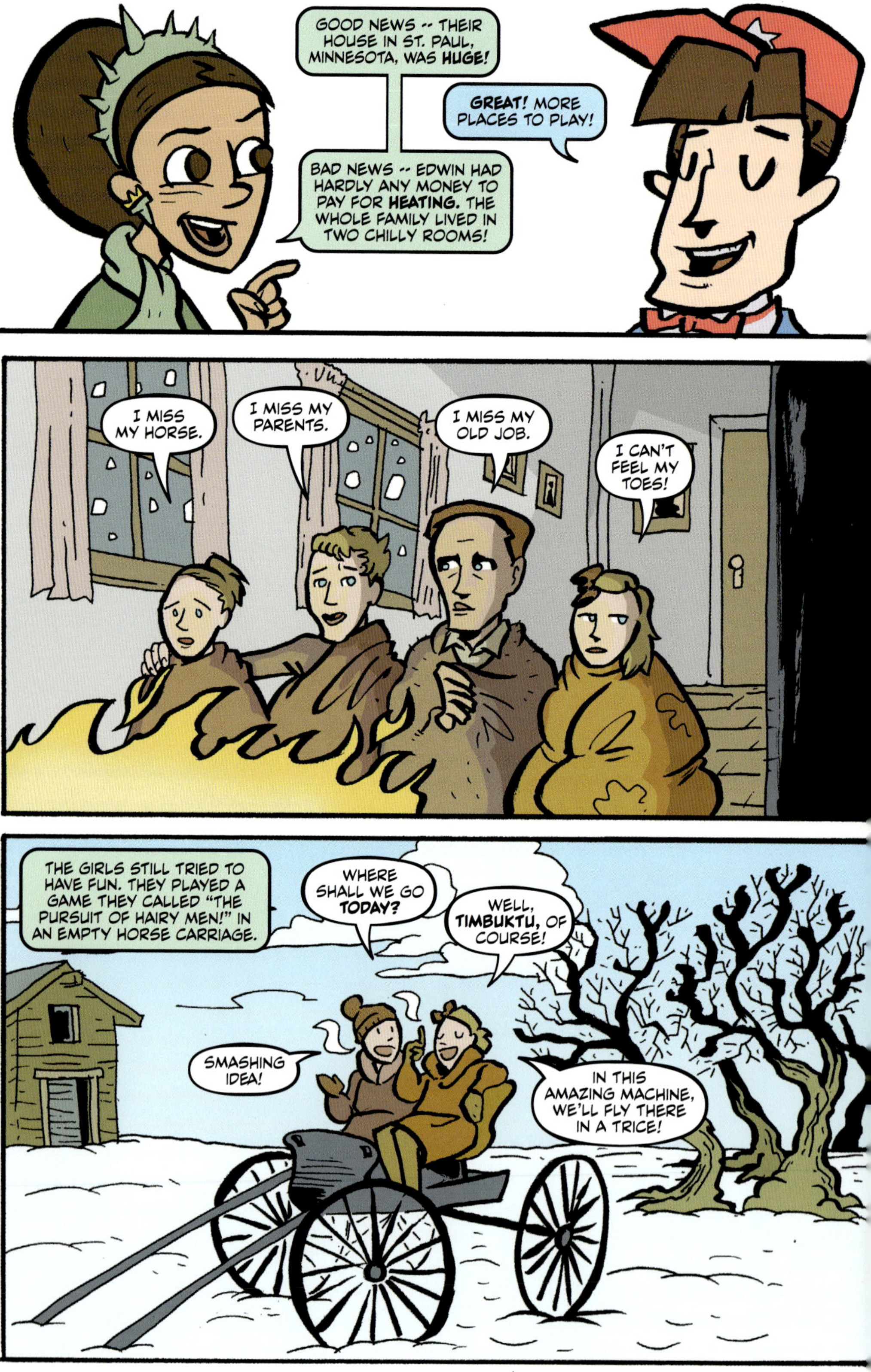
GOOD NEWS -- THEIR HOUSE IN ST. PAUL, MINNESOTA, WAS **HUGE!**
GREAT! MORE PLACES TO PLAY!
BAD NEWS -- EDWIN HAD HARDLY ANY MONEY TO PAY FOR **HEATING.** THE WHOLE FAMILY LIVED IN TWO CHILLY ROOMS!
I MISS MY HORSE.
I MISS MY PARENTS.
I MISS MY OLD JOB.
I CAN'T FEEL MY TOES!
THE GIRLS STILL TRIED TO HAVE FUN. THEY PLAYED A GAME THEY CALLED "THE PURSUIT OF HAIRY MEN!" IN AN EMPTY HORSE CARRIAGE.
WHERE SHALL WE GO **TODAY?**
WELL, **TIMBUKTU,** OF COURSE!
SMASHING IDEA!
IN THIS AMAZING MACHINE, WE'LL FLY THERE IN A TRICE!

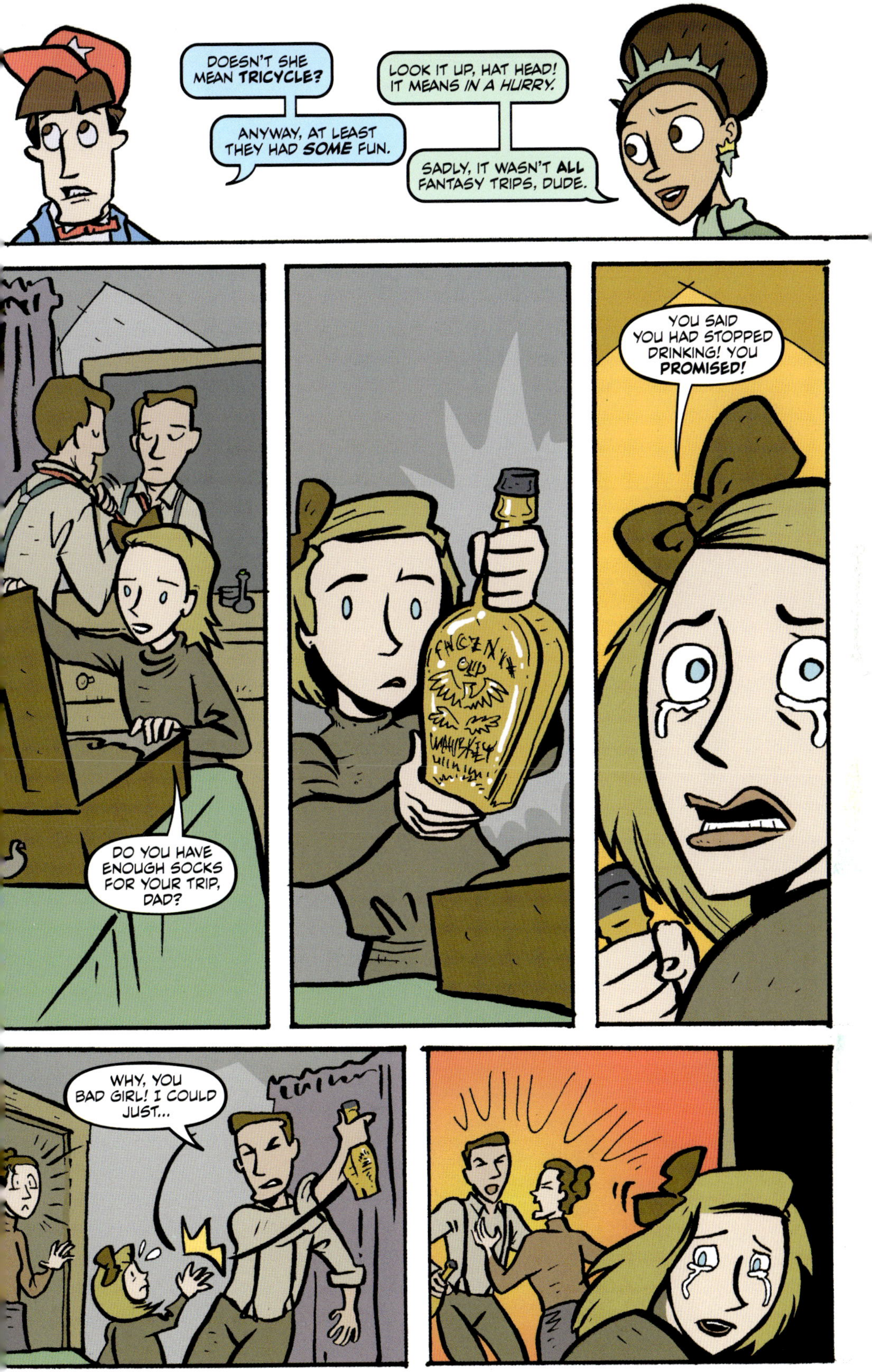
DOESN'T SHE MEAN **TRICYCLE?**
ANYWAY, AT LEAST THEY HAD **SOME** FUN.
LOOK IT UP, HAT HEAD! IT MEANS *IN A HURRY.*
SADLY, IT WASN'T **ALL** FANTASY TRIPS, DUDE.
DO YOU HAVE ENOUGH SOCKS FOR YOUR TRIP, DAD?
YOU SAID YOU HAD STOPPED DRINKING! YOU **PROMISED!**
WHY, YOU BAD GIRL! I COULD JUST...

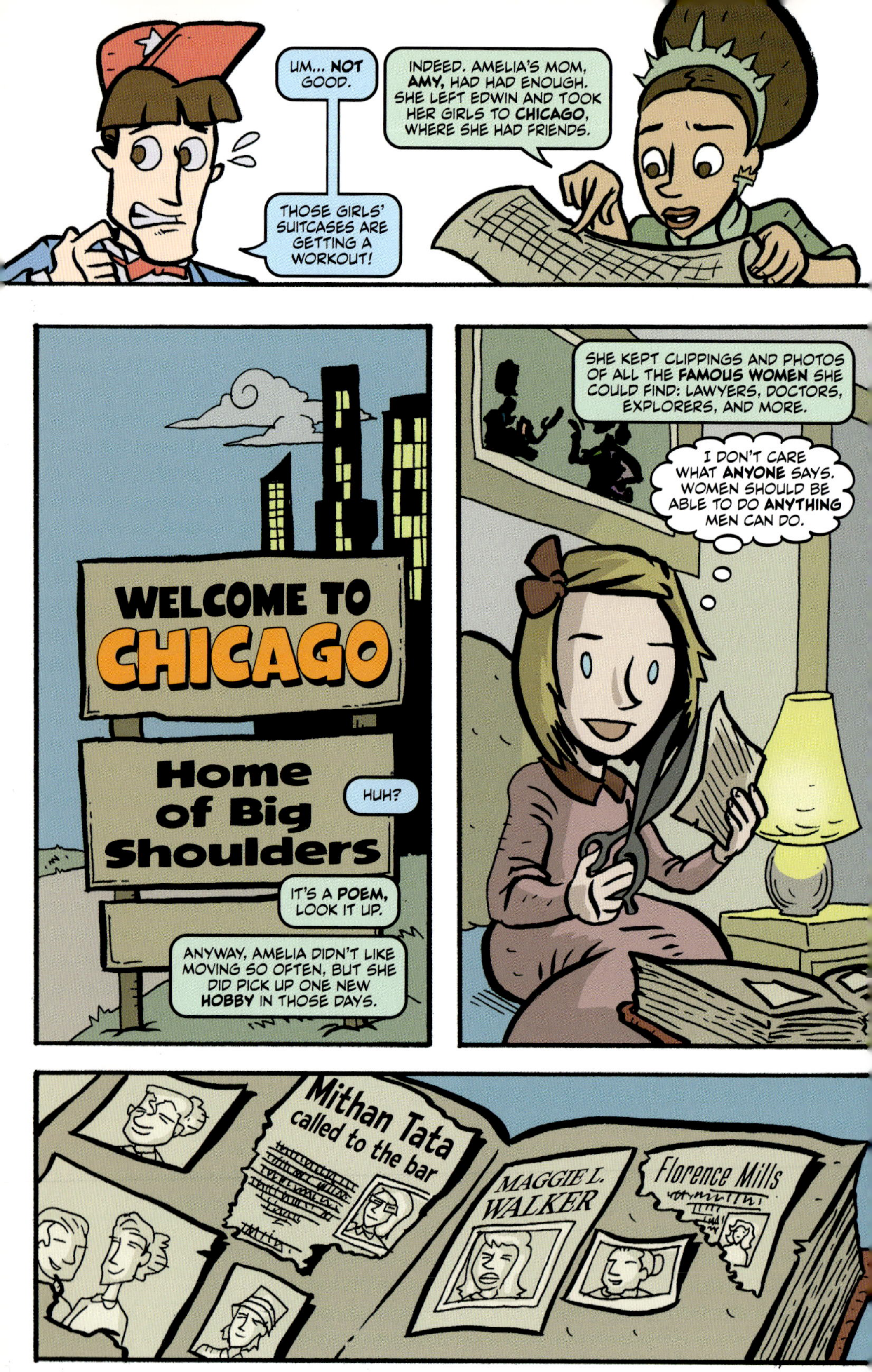
UM... **NOT** GOOD.
THOSE GIRLS' SUITCASES ARE GETTING A WORKOUT!
INDEED. AMELIA'S MOM, **AMY,** HAD HAD ENOUGH. SHE LEFT EDWIN AND TOOK HER GIRLS TO **CHICAGO,** WHERE SHE HAD FRIENDS.
WELCOME TO CHICAGO
Home of Big Shoulders
HUH?
IT'S A **POEM,** LOOK IT UP.
ANYWAY, AMELIA DIDN'T LIKE MOVING SO OFTEN, BUT SHE DID PICK UP ONE NEW **HOBBY** IN THOSE DAYS.
SHE KEPT CLIPPINGS AND PHOTOS OF ALL THE **FAMOUS WOMEN** SHE COULD FIND: LAWYERS, DOCTORS, EXPLORERS, AND MORE.
I DON'T CARE WHAT **ANYONE** SAYS. WOMEN SHOULD BE ABLE TO DO **ANYTHING** MEN CAN DO.
Mithan Tata called to the bar
MAGGIE L. WALKER
Florence Mills

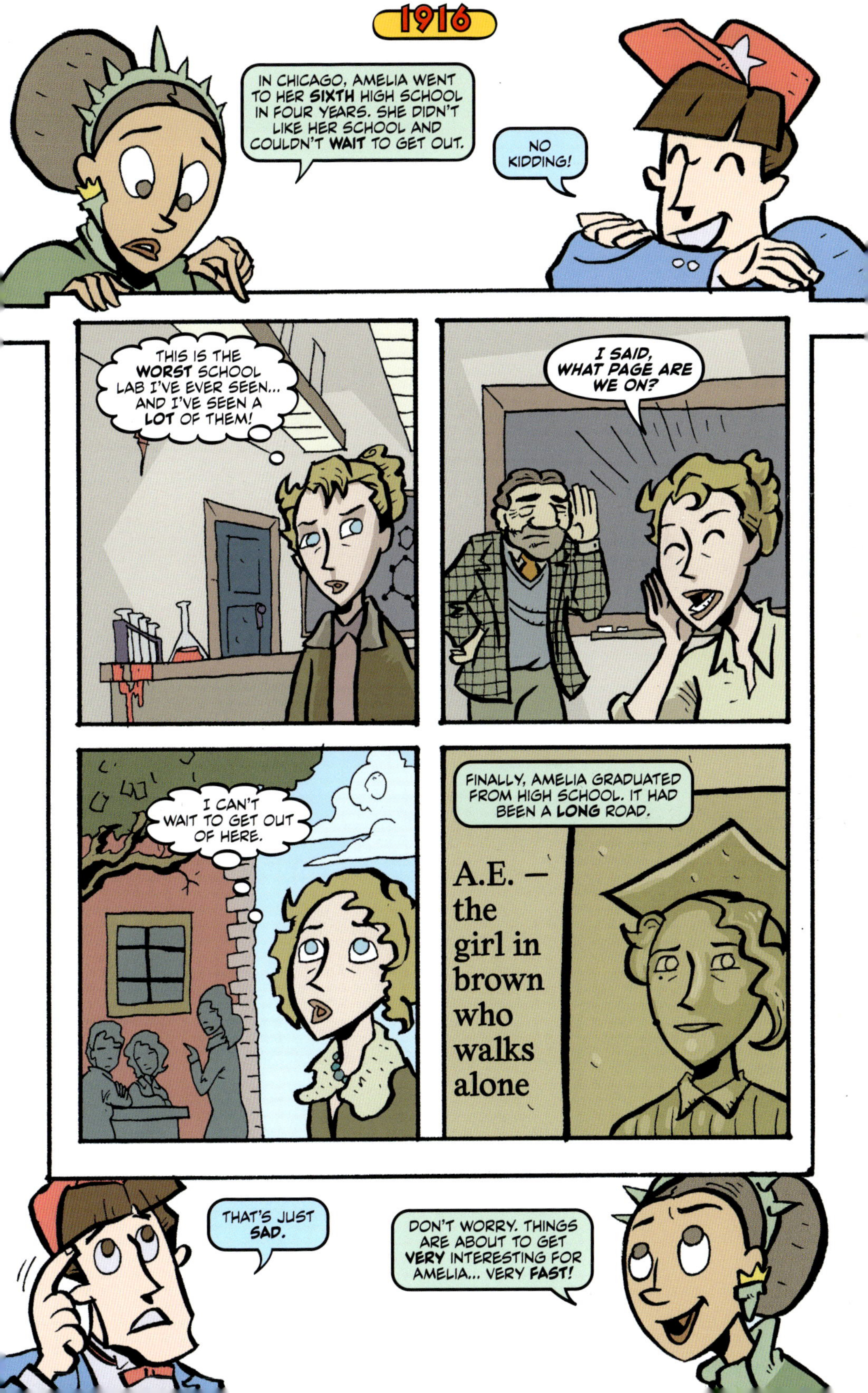
1916
IN CHICAGO, AMELIA WENT TO HER SIXTH HIGH SCHOOL IN FOUR YEARS. SHE DIDN'T LIKE HER SCHOOL AND COULDN'T WAIT TO GET OUT.
NO KIDDING!
THIS IS THE WORST SCHOOL LAB I'VE EVER SEEN... AND I'VE SEEN A LOT OF THEM!
I SAID, WHAT PAGE ARE WE ON?
I CAN'T WAIT TO GET OUT OF HERE.
FINALLY, AMELIA GRADUATED FROM HIGH SCHOOL. IT HAD BEEN A LONG ROAD.
A.E. – the girl in brown who walks alone
THAT'S JUST SAD.
DON'T WORRY. THINGS ARE ABOUT TO GET VERY INTERESTING FOR AMELIA... VERY FAST!

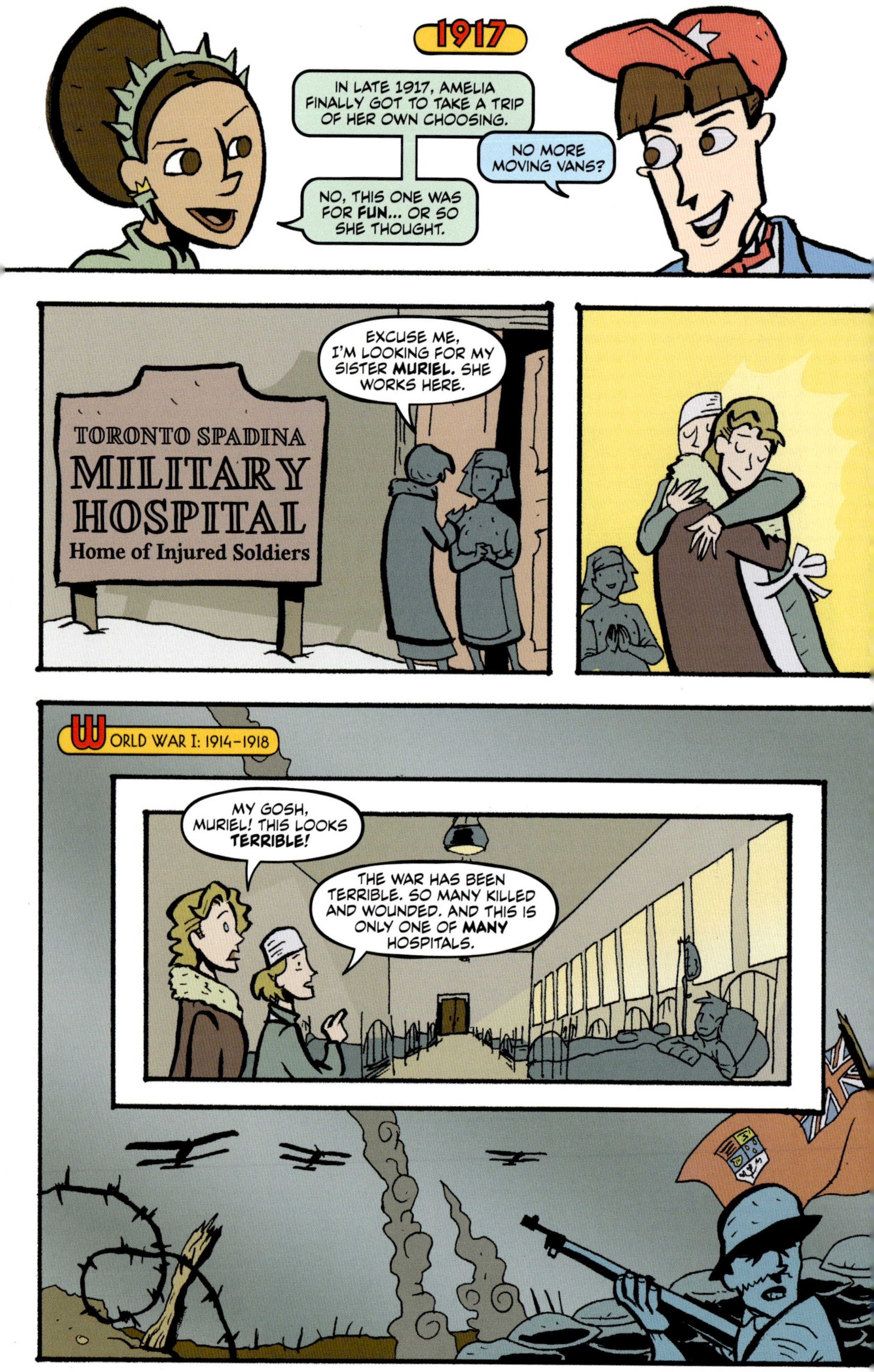
1917
IN LATE 1917, AMELIA FINALLY GOT TO TAKE A TRIP OF HER OWN CHOOSING.
NO MORE MOVING VANS?
NO, THIS ONE WAS FOR **FUN**... OR SO SHE THOUGHT.
EXCUSE ME, I'M LOOKING FOR MY SISTER **MURIEL.** SHE WORKS HERE.
TORONTO SPADINA
MILITARY HOSPITAL
Home of Injured Soldiers
WORLD WAR I: 1914–1918
MY GOSH, MURIEL! THIS LOOKS **TERRIBLE!**
THE WAR HAS BEEN TERRIBLE. SO MANY KILLED AND WOUNDED. AND THIS IS ONLY ONE OF **MANY** HOSPITALS.

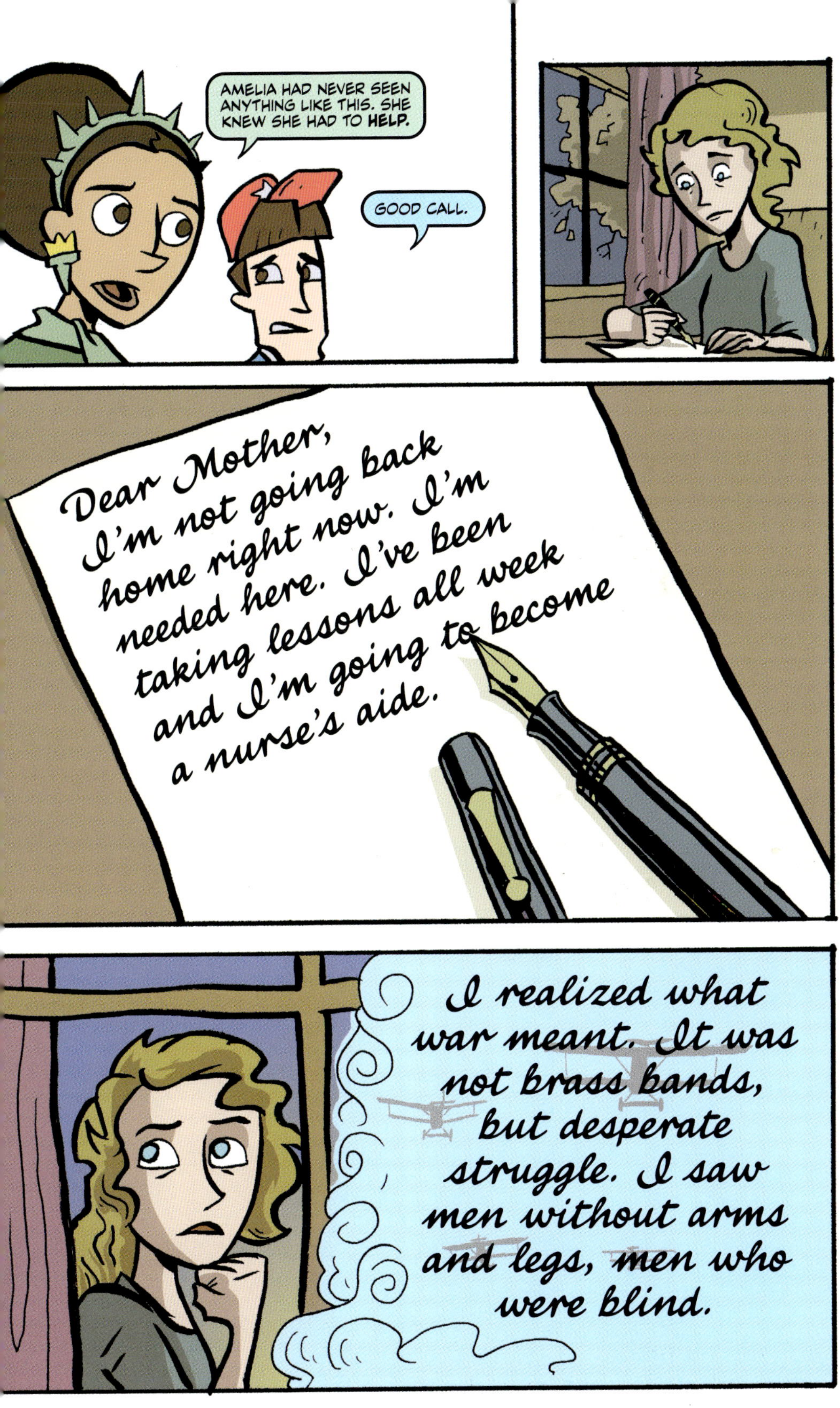
AMELIA HAD NEVER SEEN ANYTHING LIKE THIS. SHE KNEW SHE HAD TO **HELP.**
GOOD CALL.
Dear Mother,
I'm not going back home right now. I'm needed here. I've been taking lessons all week and I'm going to become a nurse's aide.
I realized what war meant. It was not brass bands, but desperate struggle. I saw men without arms and legs, men who were blind.

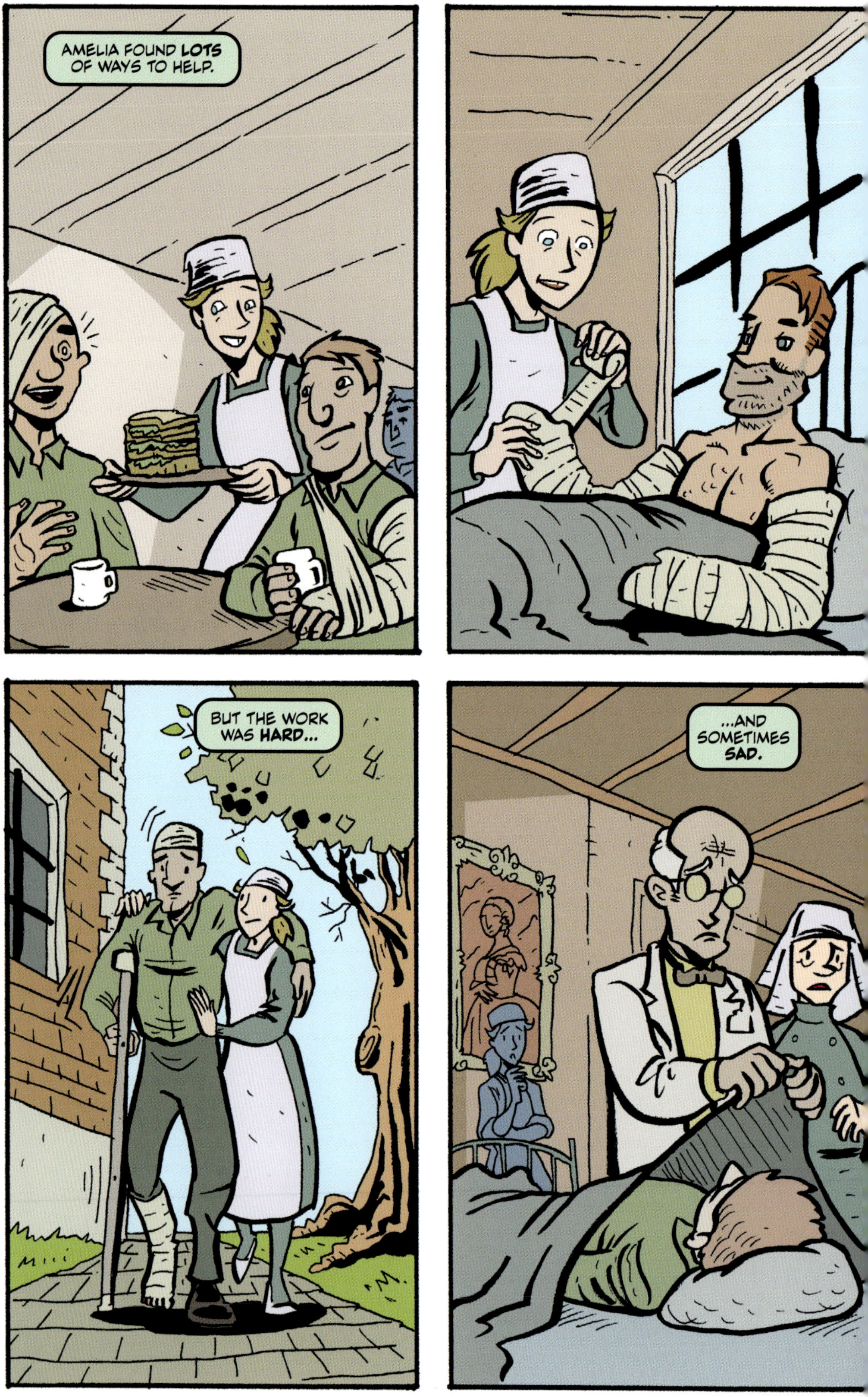
AMELIA FOUND LOTS OF WAYS TO HELP.
BUT THE WORK WAS HARD...
...AND SOMETIMES SAD.

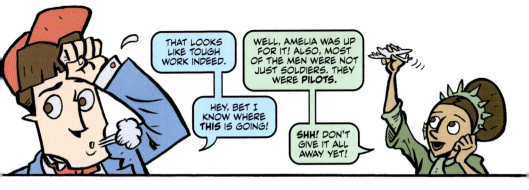

THAT LOOKS LIKE TOUGH WORK INDEED.

HEY, BET I KNOW WHERE **THIS** IS GOING!

WELL, AMELIA WAS UP FOR IT! ALSO, MOST OF THE MEN WERE NOT JUST SOLDIERS. THEY WERE **PILOTS.**

SHH! DON'T GIVE IT ALL AWAY YET!

TELL ME ABOUT YOUR JOB, SOLDIER.

I'M NO SOLDIER, NURSE. I FLY AIRPLANES. OR, THAT IS, I **DID** FLY AIRPLANES.

I'M SURE YOU WILL AGAIN, TOO. MORE SOUP?

THANKS. HAVE YOU EVER FLOWN?

I **SAW** AN AIRPLANE ONCE. DIDN'T THINK MUCH OF IT.

WELL, YOU'VE GOT TO **TRY** IT. WE'RE BEING TAKEN TO WATCH AN **AIR SHOW** THIS WEEKEND. JOIN US!

I'M NOT SURE THAT WOULD BE **PROPER.**

OKAY... THEN BRING A **FRIEND!**

OR **TWO!**

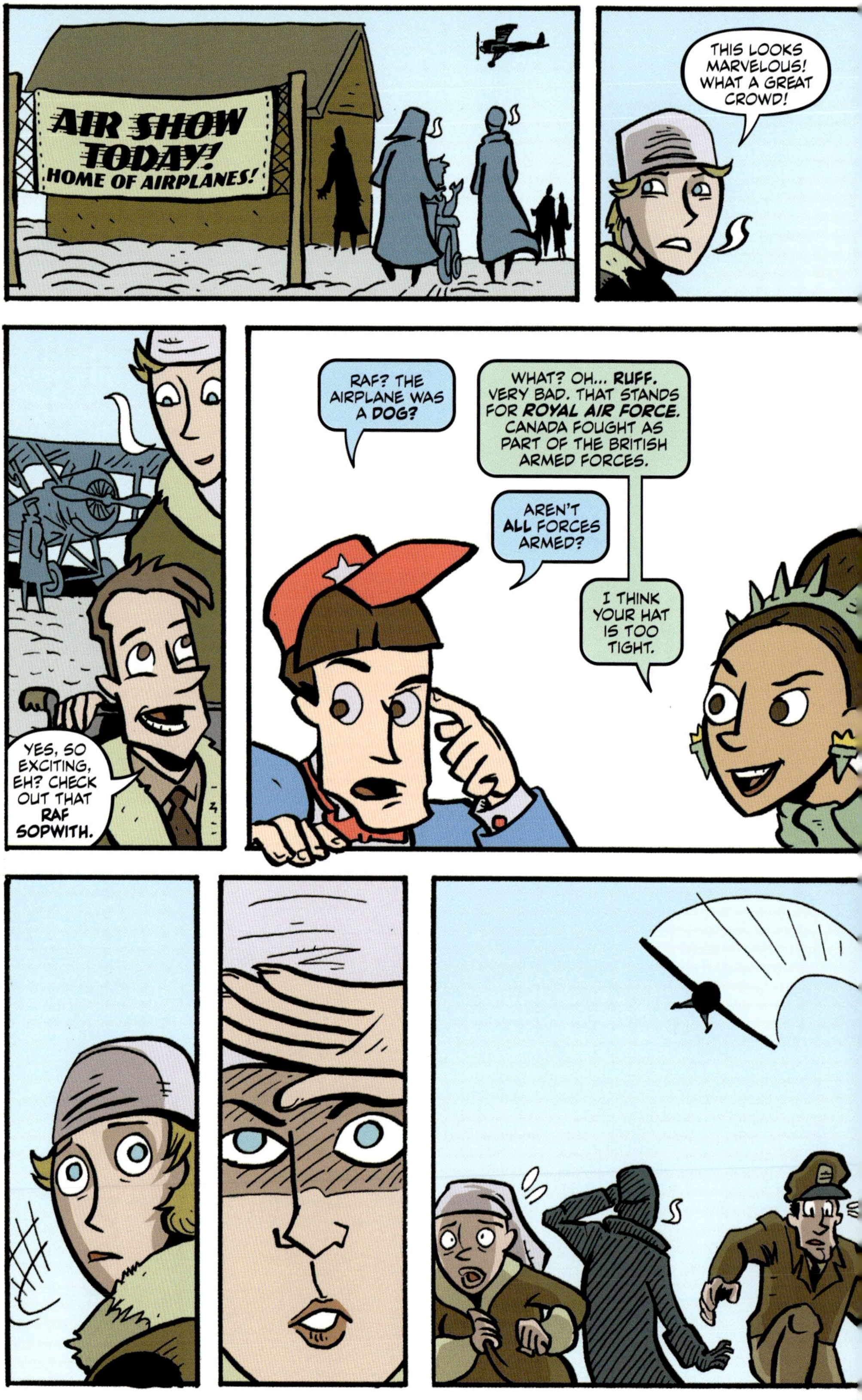
AIR SHOW TODAY! HOME OF AIRPLANES!
THIS LOOKS MARVELOUS! WHAT A GREAT CROWD!
YES, SO EXCITING, EH? CHECK OUT THAT **RAF SOPWITH.**
RAF? THE AIRPLANE WAS A **DOG?**
WHAT? OH... **RUFF.** VERY BAD. THAT STANDS FOR ***ROYAL AIR FORCE.*** CANADA FOUGHT AS PART OF THE BRITISH ARMED FORCES.
AREN'T **ALL** FORCES ARMED?
I THINK YOUR HAT IS TOO TIGHT.

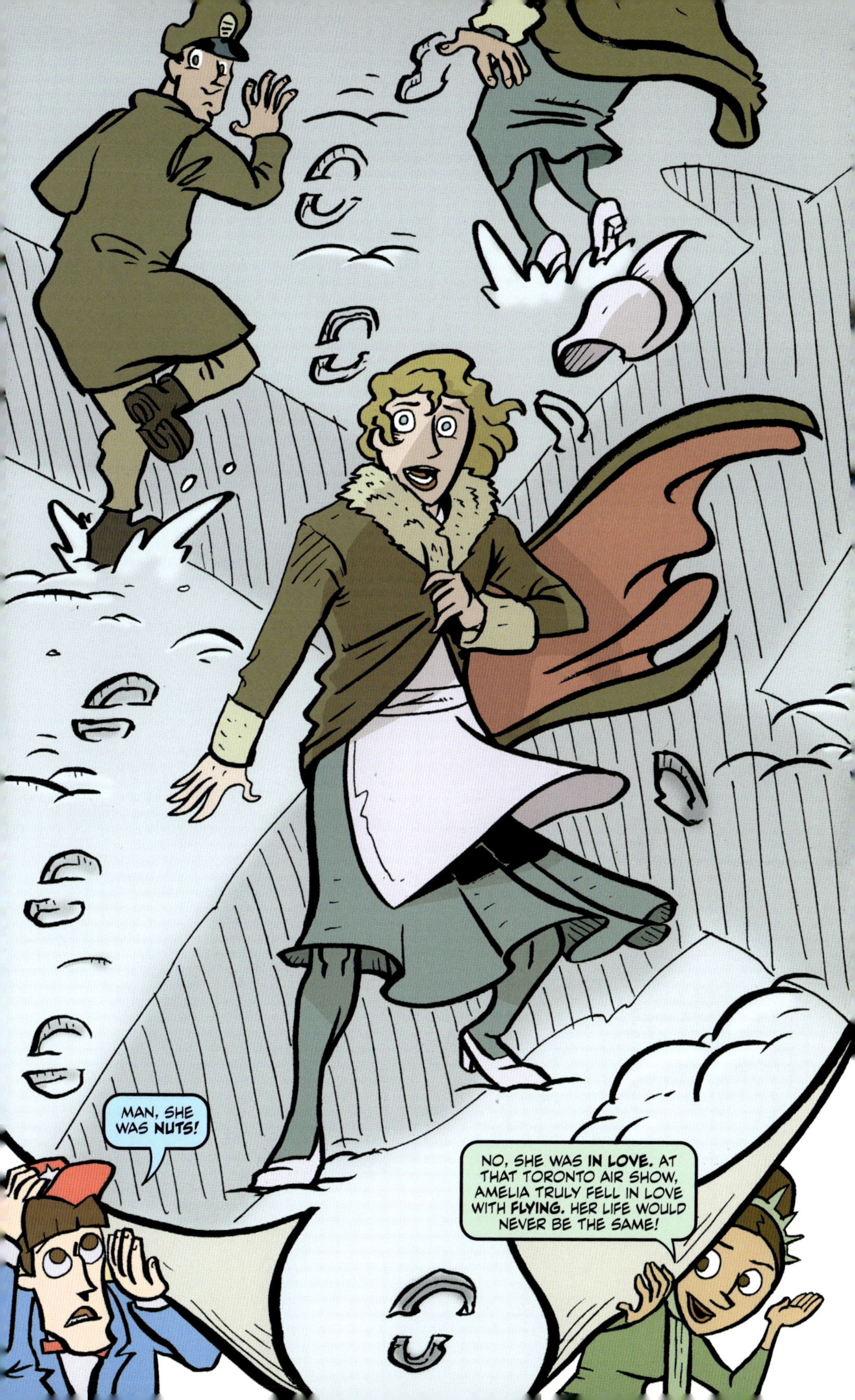
MAN, SHE WAS **NUTS!**
NO, SHE WAS **IN LOVE.** AT THAT TORONTO AIR SHOW, AMELIA TRULY FELL IN LOVE WITH **FLYING.** HER LIFE WOULD NEVER BE THE SAME!

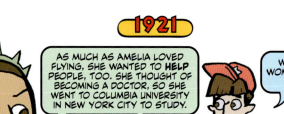

AS MUCH AS AMELIA LOVED FLYING, SHE WANTED TO **HELP** PEOPLE, TOO. SHE THOUGHT OF BECOMING A DOCTOR, SO SHE WENT TO COLUMBIA UNIVERSITY IN NEW YORK CITY TO STUDY.

OF COURSE! JUST NOT VERY MANY, SO IT WAS **ANOTHER** BOLD MOVE FOR AMELIA.

WERE THERE WOMEN DOCTORS THEN?

MY BROTHER JOHN FLEW AIRPLANES IN THE WAR. I THINK THAT WOULD BE EVER SO **EXCITING!**

I DON'T KNOW. I THINK I'D BE **AFRAID** TO BE UP THAT HIGH.

NOT **ME!** I LOVE THE IDEA OF FLYING. I'M GOING TO TAKE **LESSONS** AS SOON AS I CAN.

AMELIA, DON'T YOU DARE! IT'S SO **DANGEROUS!**

AND THE **HEIGHTS!** I CAN'T EVEN LOOK OUT A HIGH WINDOW WITHOUT BEING DIZZY.

HEIGHTS DON'T BOTHER ME AT ALL.

IN FACT, I'LL **PROVE** IT TO YOU!

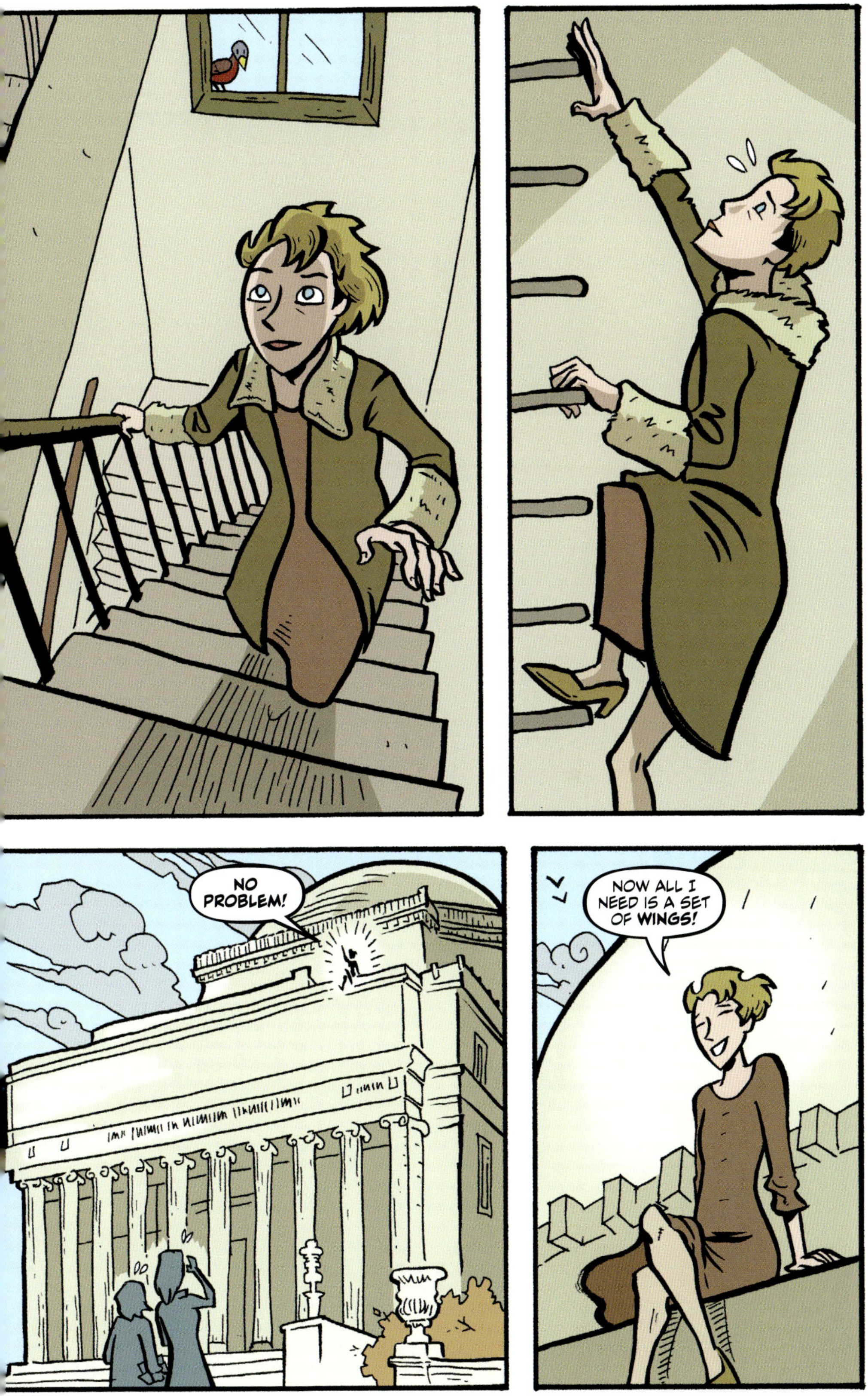
NO PROBLEM!
NOW ALL I NEED IS A SET OF WINGS!

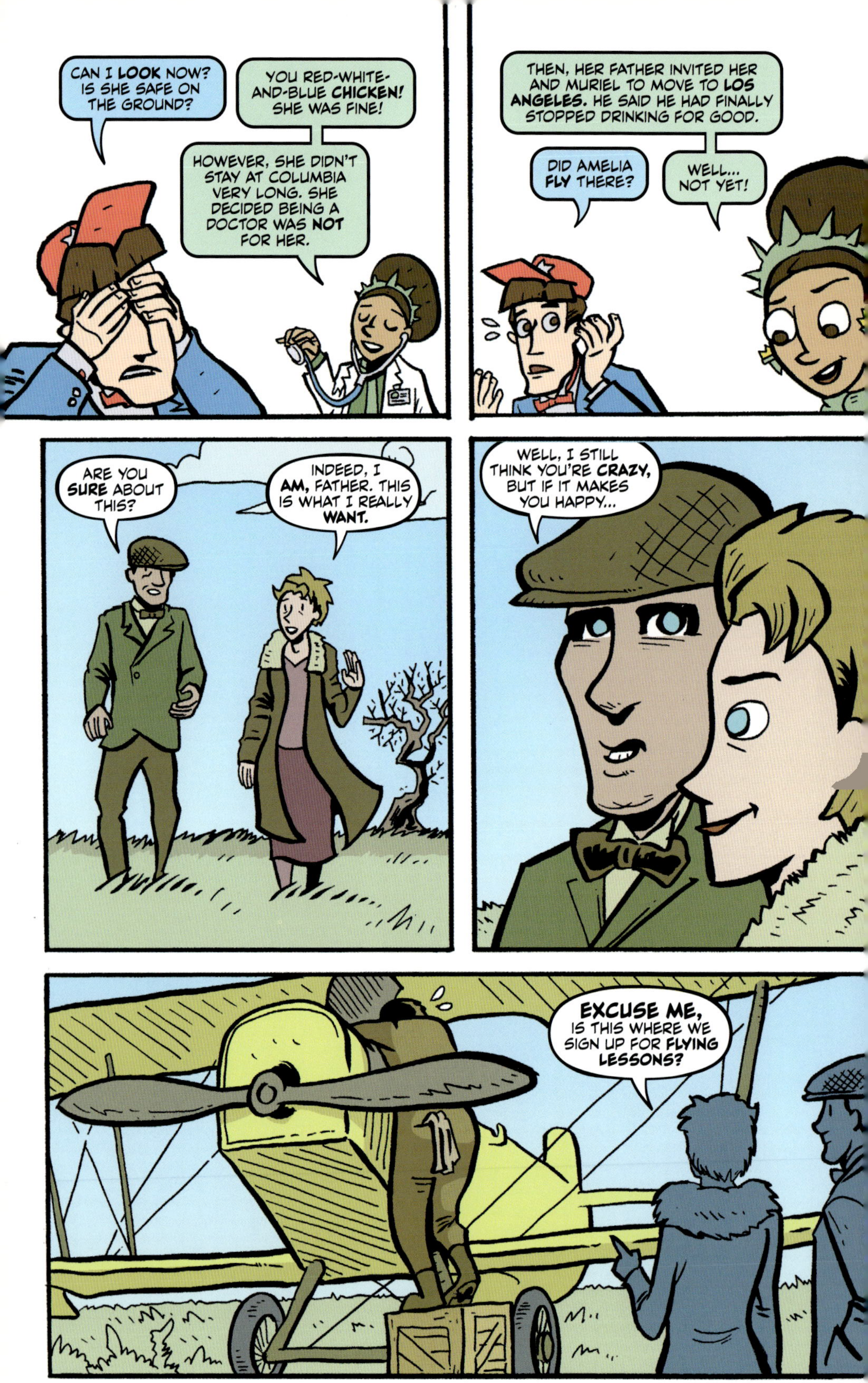
CAN I LOOK NOW? IS SHE SAFE ON THE GROUND?
YOU RED-WHITE-AND-BLUE CHICKEN! SHE WAS FINE!
HOWEVER, SHE DIDN'T STAY AT COLUMBIA VERY LONG. SHE DECIDED BEING A DOCTOR WAS NOT FOR HER.
THEN, HER FATHER INVITED HER AND MURIEL TO MOVE TO LOS ANGELES. HE SAID HE HAD FINALLY STOPPED DRINKING FOR GOOD.
DID AMELIA FLY THERE?
WELL... NOT YET!
ARE YOU SURE ABOUT THIS?
INDEED, I AM, FATHER. THIS IS WHAT I REALLY WANT.
WELL, I STILL THINK YOU'RE CRAZY, BUT IF IT MAKES YOU HAPPY...
EXCUSE ME, IS THIS WHERE WE SIGN UP FOR FLYING LESSONS?

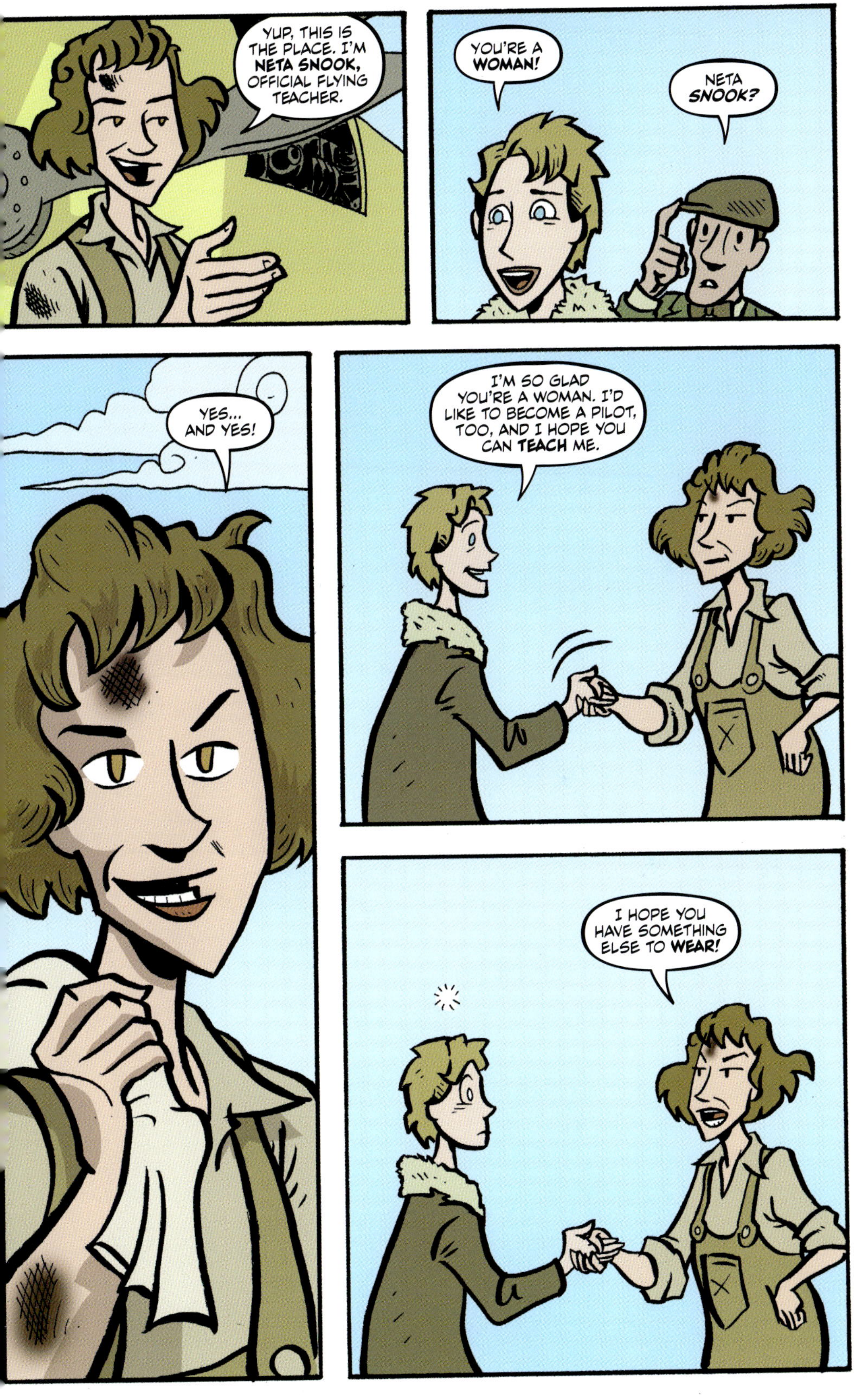
YUP, THIS IS THE PLACE. I'M NETA SNOOK, OFFICIAL FLYING TEACHER.
YOU'RE A WOMAN!
NETA SNOOK?
YES... AND YES!
I'M SO GLAD YOU'RE A WOMAN. I'D LIKE TO BECOME A PILOT, TOO, AND I HOPE YOU CAN TEACH ME.
I HOPE YOU HAVE SOMETHING ELSE TO WEAR!

WELL, I HOPE YOU LEFT **SOMETHING** IN THE PILOTS' STORE FOR EVERYONE ELSE!

WHAT? TOO MUCH?

WELL, RIGHT NOW, YOU'D MAKE A GREAT **MODEL.**

LET'S SEE IF WE CAN PUT THOSE **FANCY CLOTHES** TO USE!

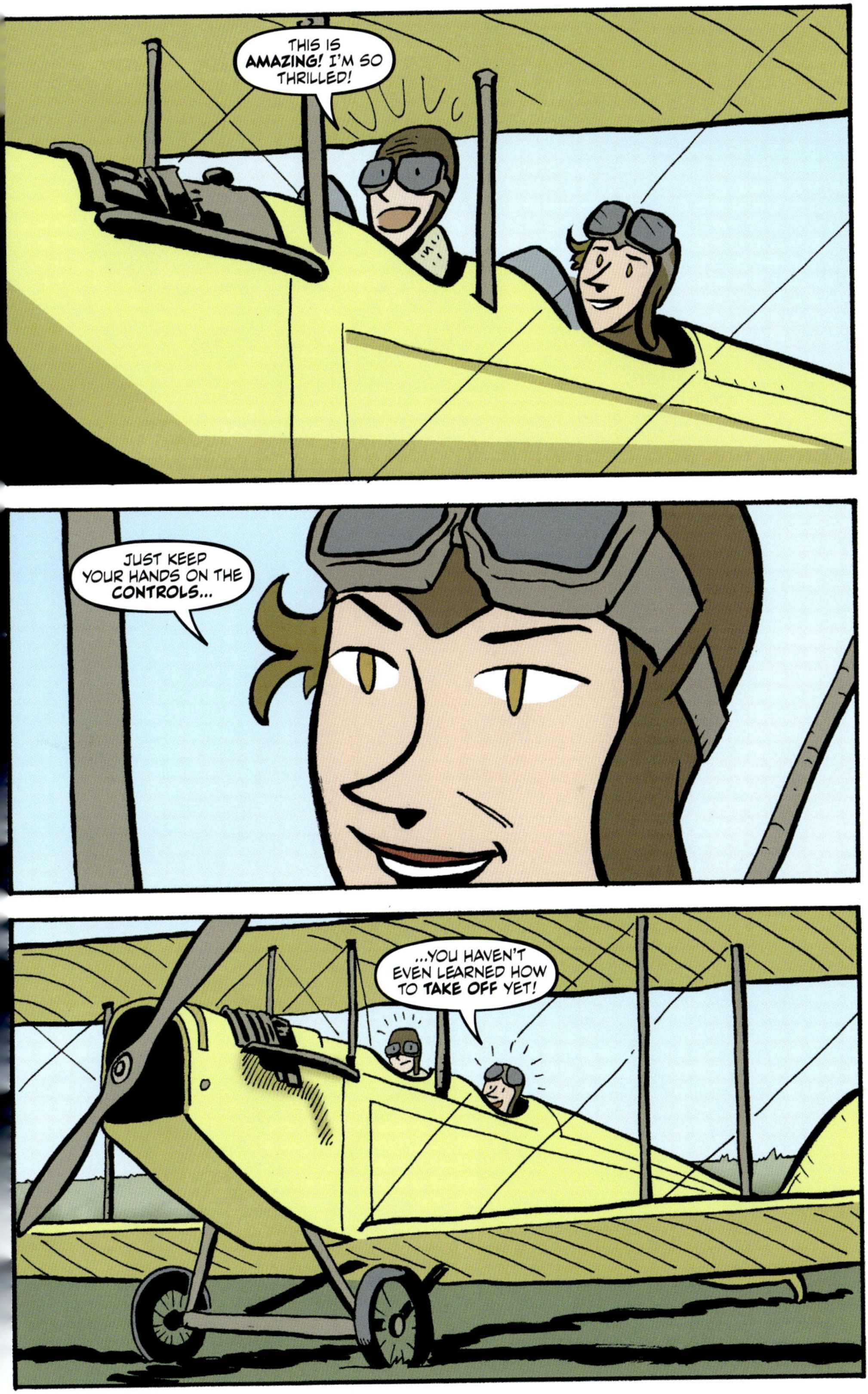
THIS IS AMAZING! I'M SO THRILLED!
JUST KEEP YOUR HANDS ON THE CONTROLS...
...YOU HAVEN'T EVEN LEARNED HOW TO TAKE OFF YET!

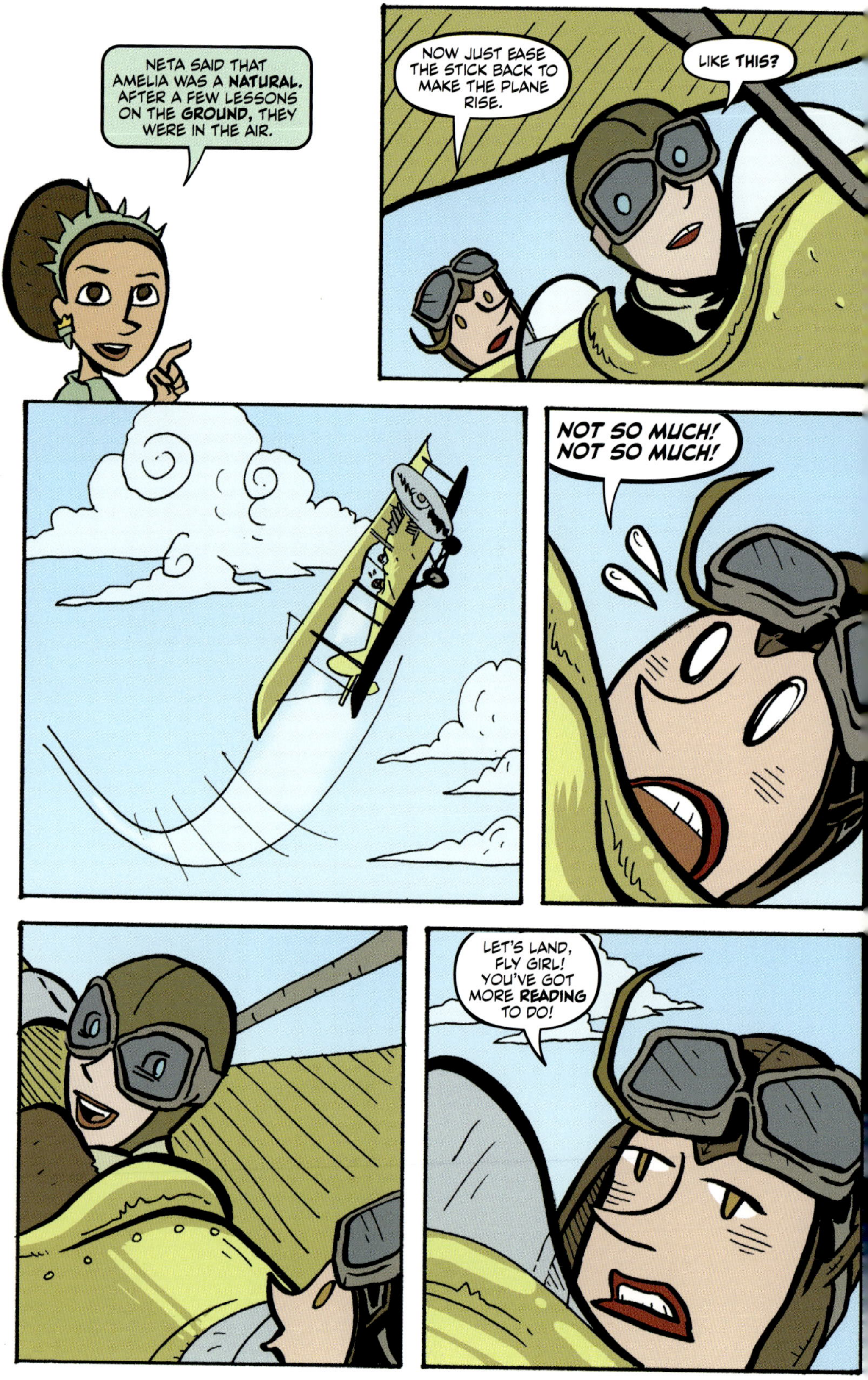
NETA SAID THAT AMELIA WAS A **NATURAL.** AFTER A FEW LESSONS ON THE **GROUND,** THEY WERE IN THE AIR.
NOW JUST EASE THE STICK BACK TO MAKE THE PLANE RISE.
LIKE **THIS?**
NOT SO MUCH! NOT SO MUCH!
LET'S LAND, FLY GIRL! YOU'VE GOT MORE **READING** TO DO!

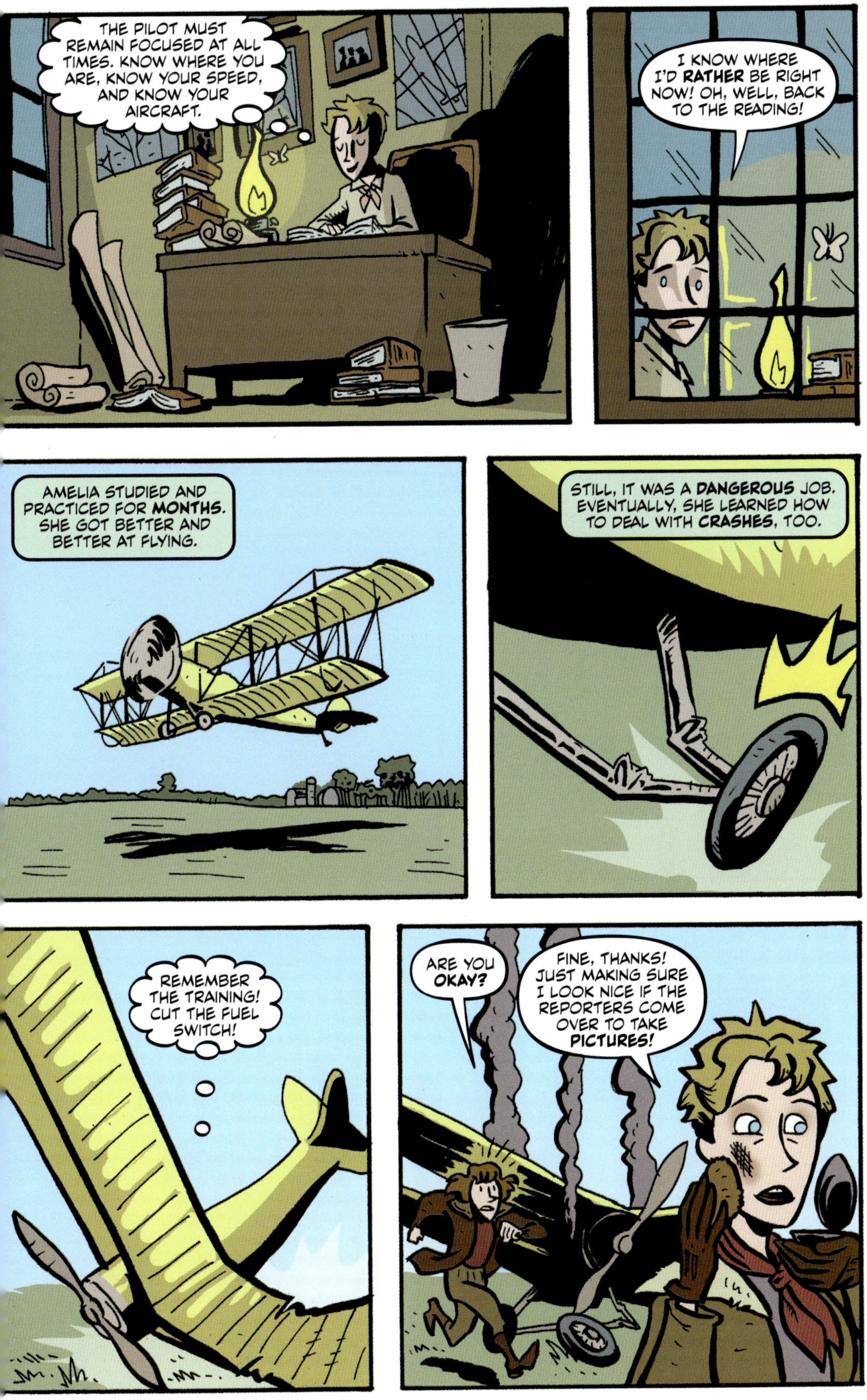
THE PILOT MUST REMAIN FOCUSED AT ALL TIMES. KNOW WHERE YOU ARE, KNOW YOUR SPEED, AND KNOW YOUR AIRCRAFT.
I KNOW WHERE I'D RATHER BE RIGHT NOW! OH, WELL, BACK TO THE READING!
AMELIA STUDIED AND PRACTICED FOR MONTHS. SHE GOT BETTER AND BETTER AT FLYING.
STILL, IT WAS A DANGEROUS JOB. EVENTUALLY, SHE LEARNED HOW TO DEAL WITH CRASHES, TOO.
REMEMBER THE TRAINING! CUT THE FUEL SWITCH!
ARE YOU OKAY?
FINE, THANKS! JUST MAKING SURE I LOOK NICE IF THE REPORTERS COME OVER TO TAKE PICTURES!

SO WHEN DID SHE FLY ACROSS THE OCEAN?

LET'S GO, WHILE WE'RE **YOUNG!**

YOU'RE SO **IMPATIENT!** WHAT'S THE RUSH?

SHH! AMELIA'S GOT A DRIVING JOB TO EARN MONEY.

ANOTHER DAY, ANOTHER DOLLAR. PRETTY SOON, I'LL HAVE ENOUGH FOR MY OWN **AIRPLANE!**

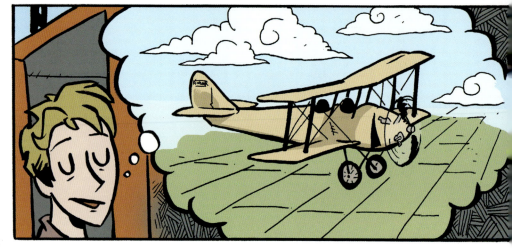

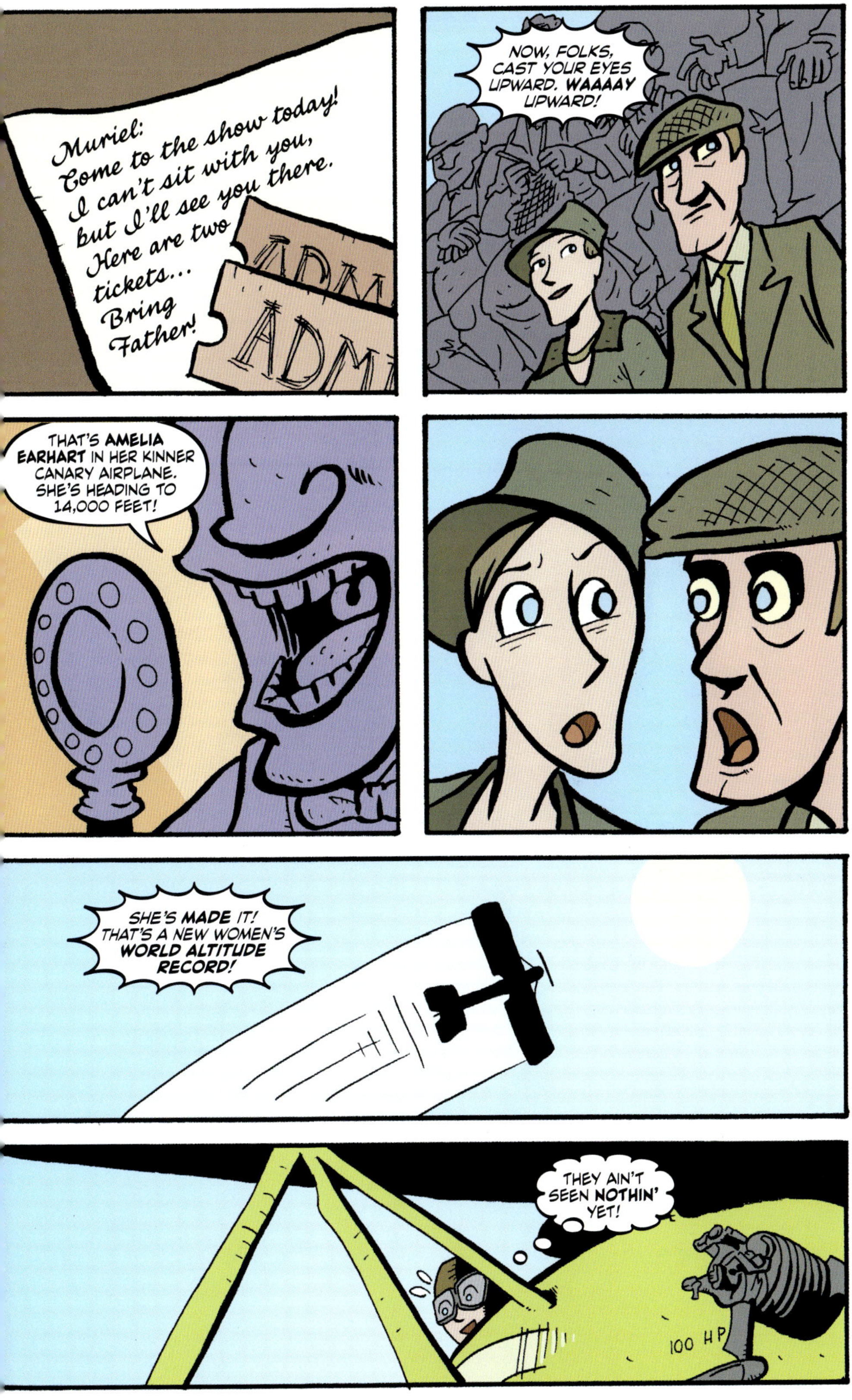
Muriel:
Come to the show today!
I can't sit with you,
but I'll see you there.
Here are two
tickets...
Bring
Father!
NOW, FOLKS, CAST YOUR EYES UPWARD. WAAAAY UPWARD!
THAT'S AMELIA EARHART IN HER KINNER CANARY AIRPLANE. SHE'S HEADING TO 14,000 FEET!
SHE'S MADE IT! THAT'S A NEW WOMEN'S WORLD ALTITUDE RECORD!
THEY AIN'T SEEN NOTHIN' YET!
100 HP

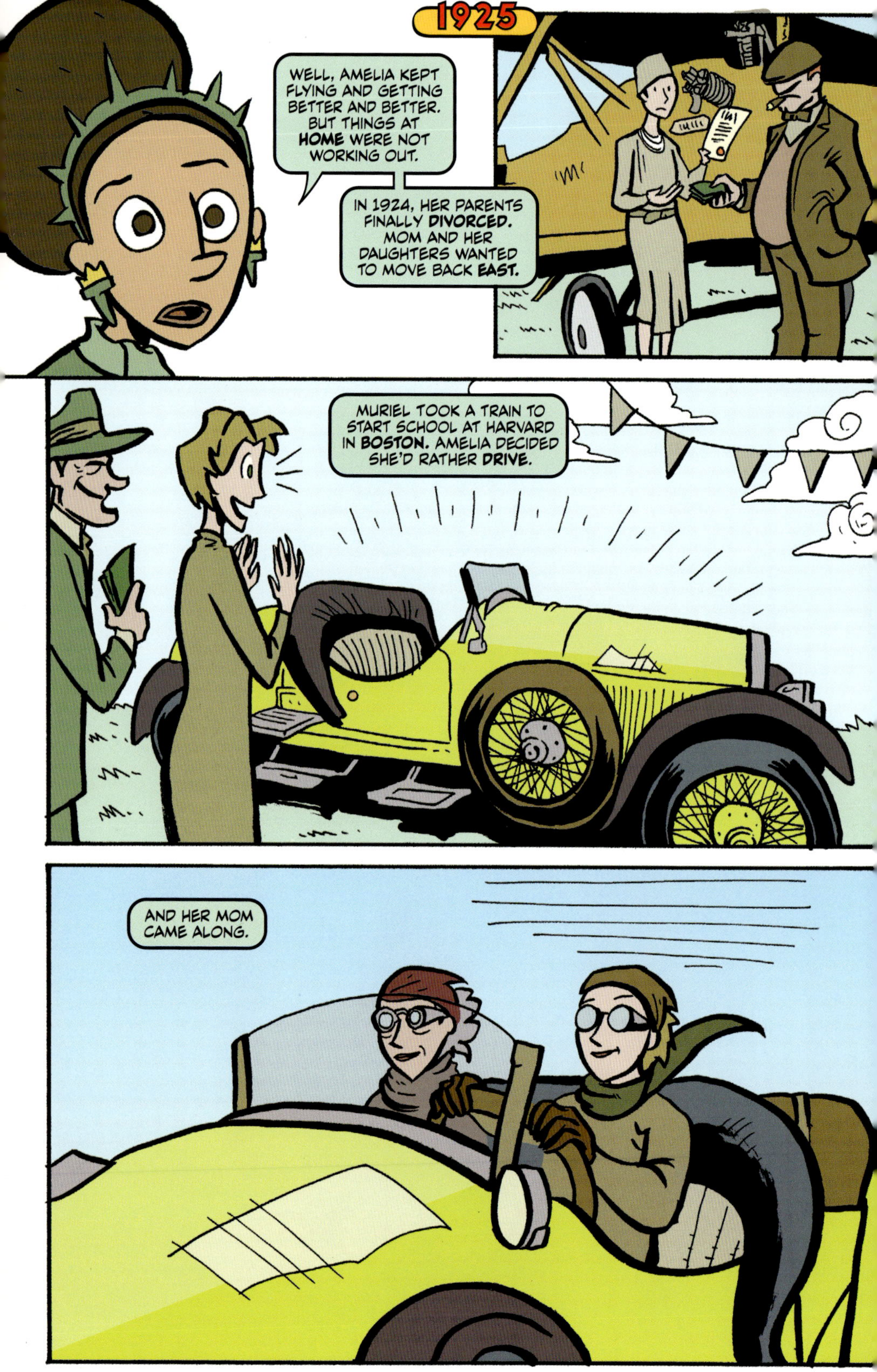
1925
WELL, AMELIA KEPT FLYING AND GETTING BETTER AND BETTER. BUT THINGS AT **HOME** WERE NOT WORKING OUT.
IN 1924, HER PARENTS FINALLY **DIVORCED.** MOM AND HER DAUGHTERS WANTED TO MOVE BACK **EAST.**
MURIEL TOOK A TRAIN TO START SCHOOL AT HARVARD IN **BOSTON.** AMELIA DECIDED SHE'D RATHER **DRIVE.**
AND HER MOM CAME ALONG.

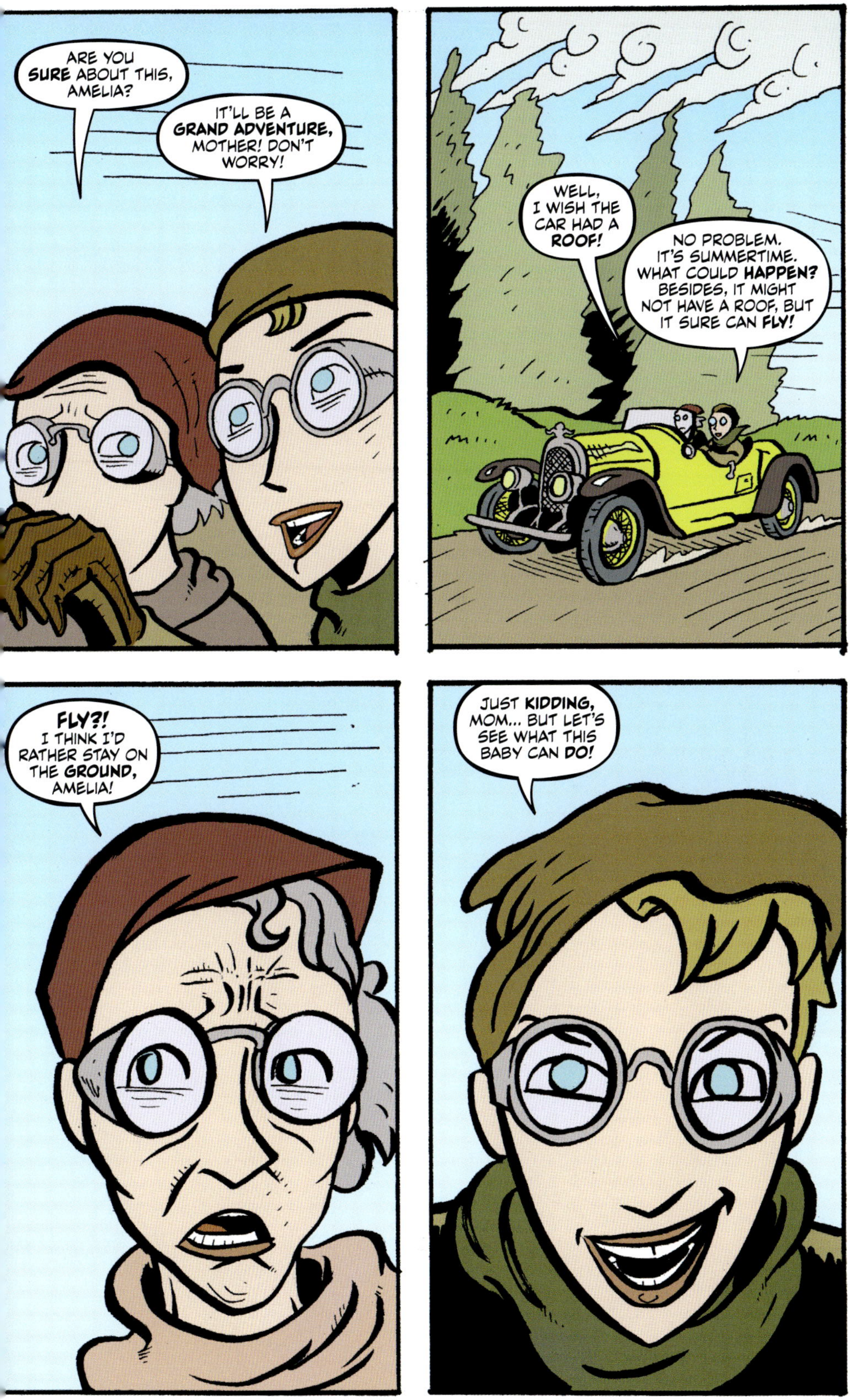
ARE YOU SURE ABOUT THIS, AMELIA?
IT'LL BE A GRAND ADVENTURE, MOTHER! DON'T WORRY!
WELL, I WISH THE CAR HAD A ROOF!
NO PROBLEM. IT'S SUMMERTIME. WHAT COULD HAPPEN? BESIDES, IT MIGHT NOT HAVE A ROOF, BUT IT SURE CAN FLY!
FLY?! I THINK I'D RATHER STAY ON THE GROUND, AMELIA!
JUST KIDDING, MOM... BUT LET'S SEE WHAT THIS BABY CAN DO!

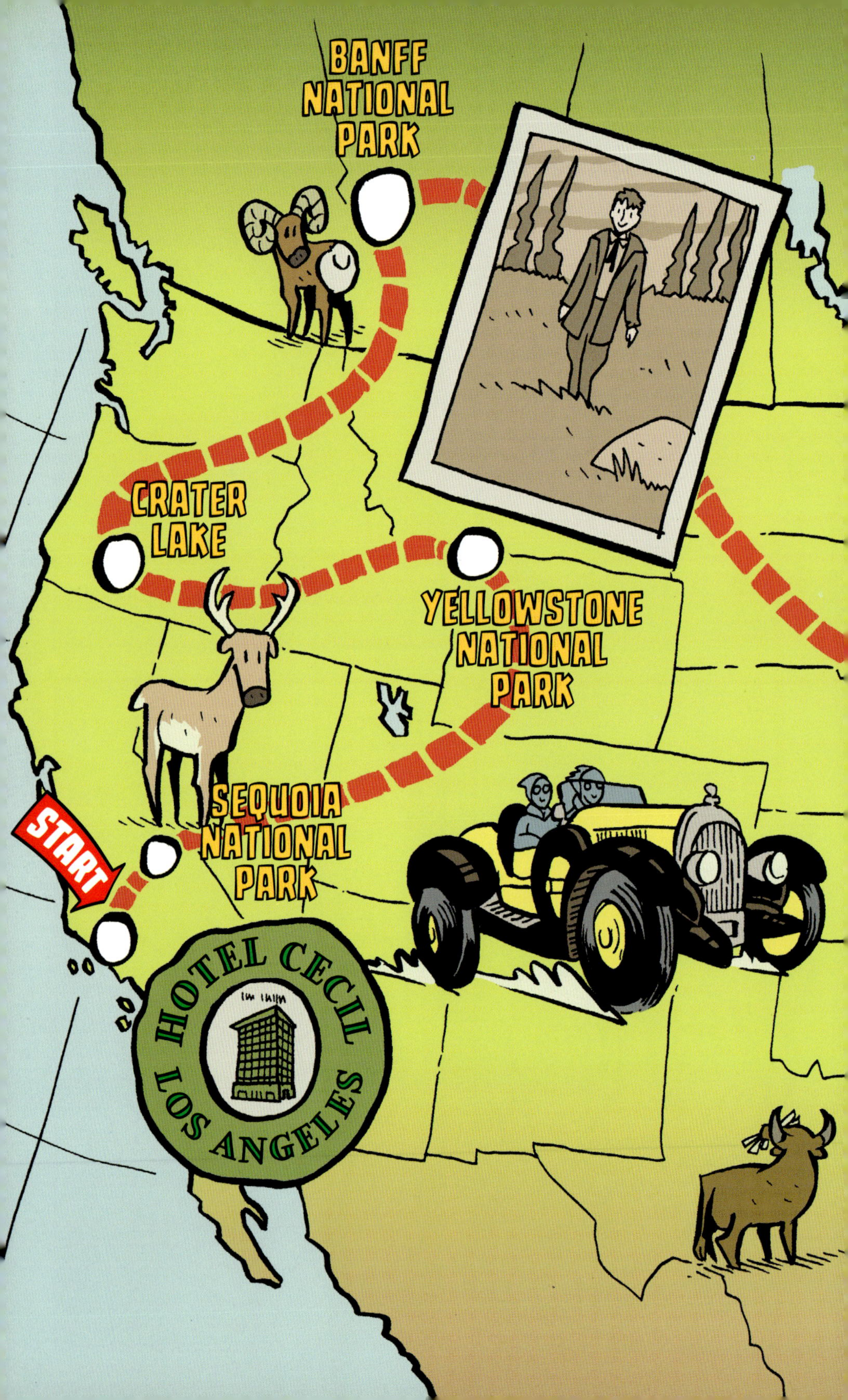
BANFF NATIONAL PARK
CRATER LAKE
YELLOWSTONE NATIONAL PARK
SEQUOIA NATIONAL PARK
START
HOTEL CECIL LOS ANGELES

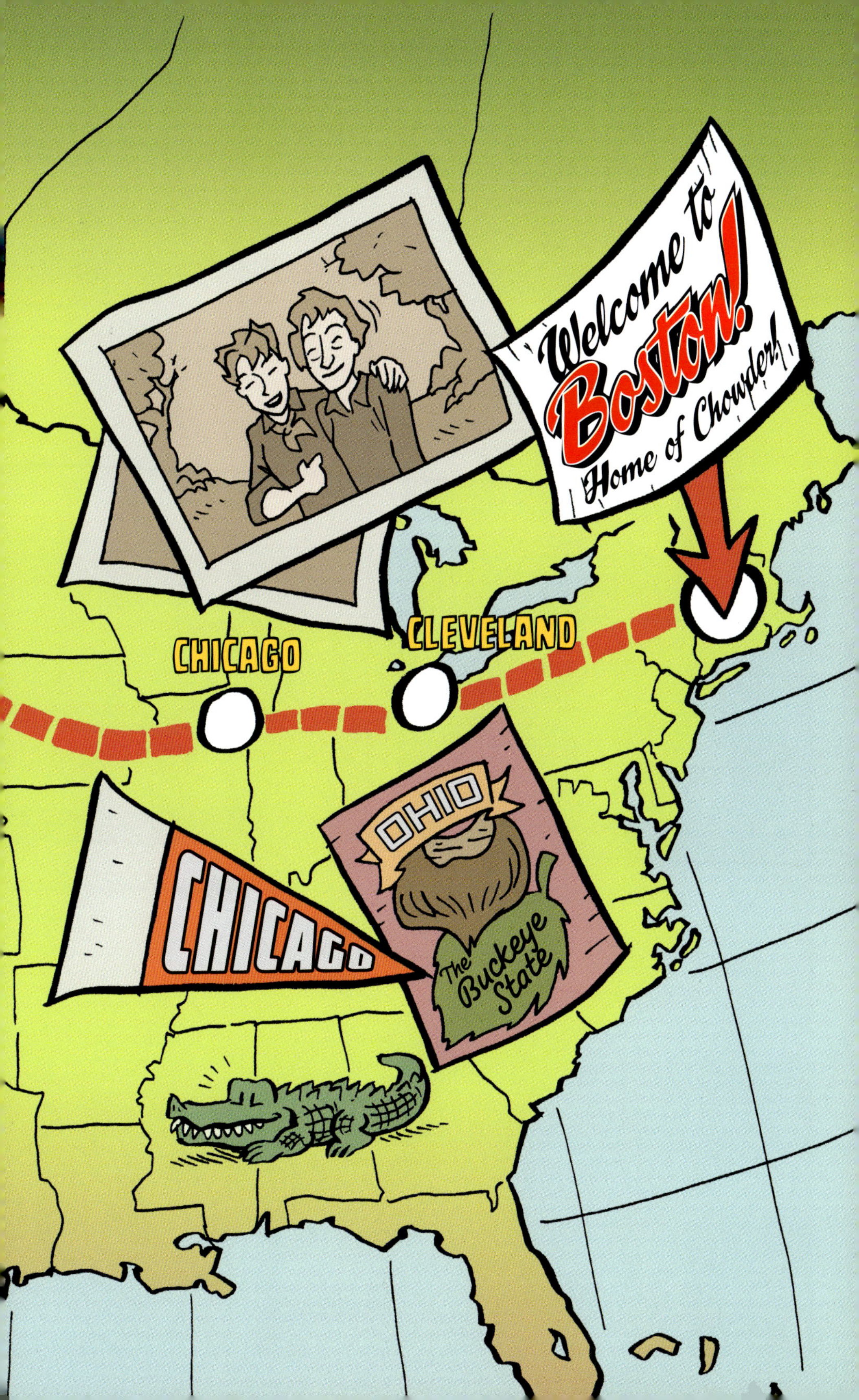
Welcome to
Boston!
Home of Chowder!
CHICAGO
CLEVELAND
OHIO
The Buckeye State
CHICAGO

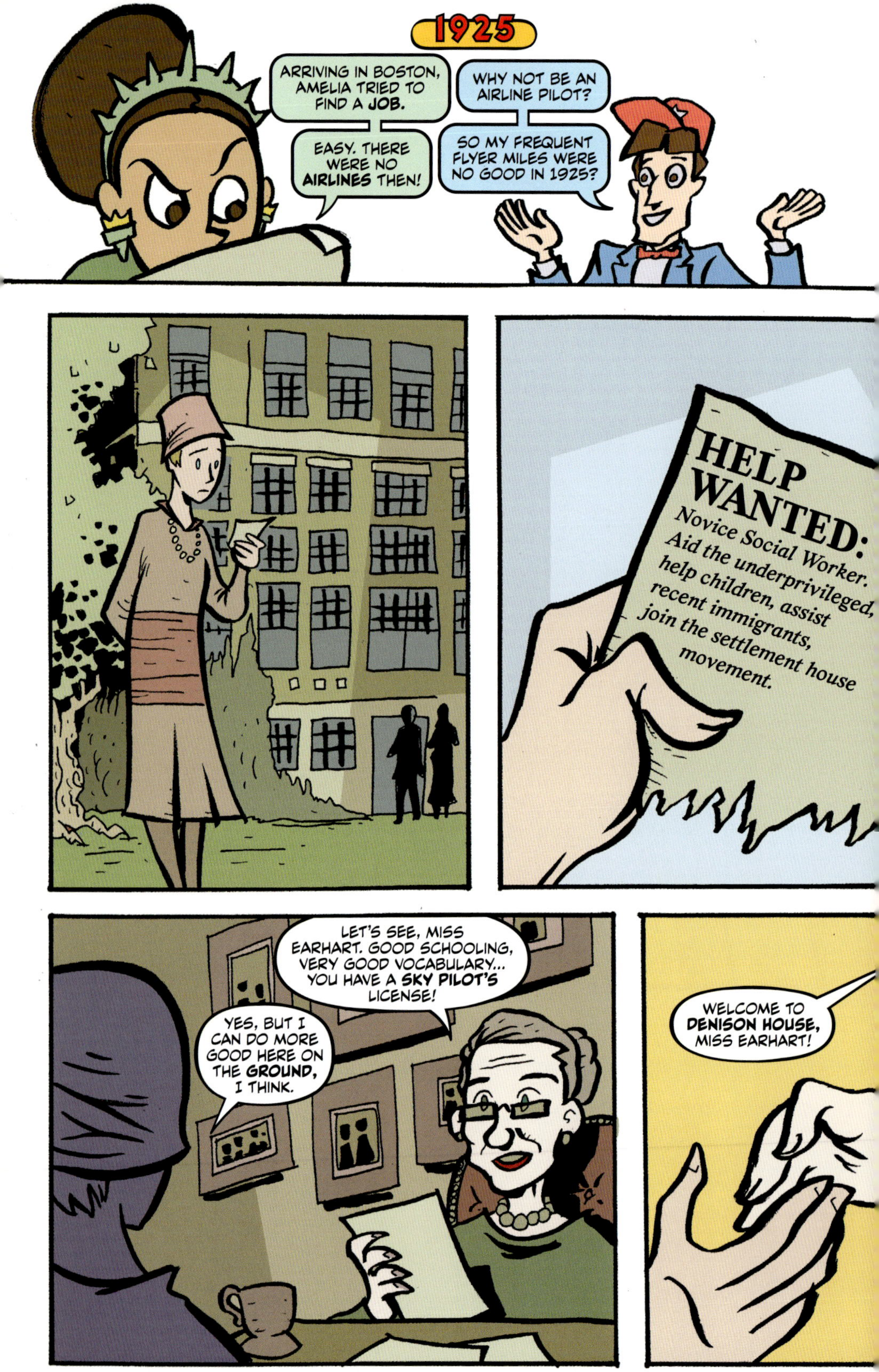
1925
ARRIVING IN BOSTON, AMELIA TRIED TO FIND A JOB.
EASY. THERE WERE NO AIRLINES THEN!
WHY NOT BE AN AIRLINE PILOT?
SO MY FREQUENT FLYER MILES WERE NO GOOD IN 1925?
HELP WANTED:
Novice Social Worker. Aid the underprivileged, help children, assist recent immigrants, join the settlement house movement.
LET'S SEE, MISS EARHART. GOOD SCHOOLING, VERY GOOD VOCABULARY... YOU HAVE A SKY PILOT'S LICENSE!
YES, BUT I CAN DO MORE GOOD HERE ON THE GROUND, I THINK.
WELCOME TO DENISON HOUSE, MISS EARHART!

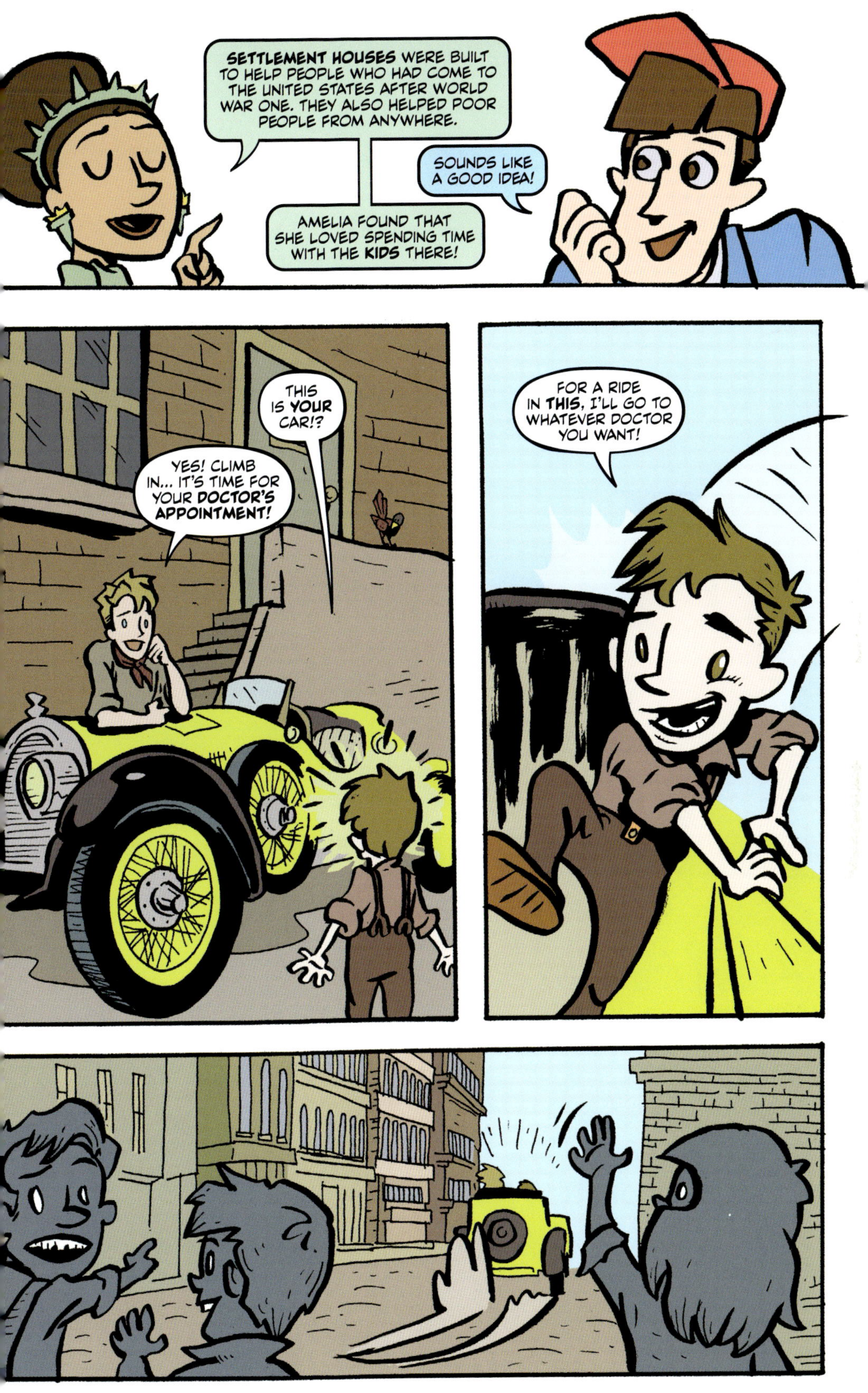
SETTLEMENT HOUSES WERE BUILT TO HELP PEOPLE WHO HAD COME TO THE UNITED STATES AFTER WORLD WAR ONE. THEY ALSO HELPED POOR PEOPLE FROM ANYWHERE.
AMELIA FOUND THAT SHE LOVED SPENDING TIME WITH THE KIDS THERE!
SOUNDS LIKE A GOOD IDEA!
YES! CLIMB IN... IT'S TIME FOR YOUR DOCTOR'S APPOINTMENT!
THIS IS YOUR CAR!?
FOR A RIDE IN THIS, I'LL GO TO WHATEVER DOCTOR YOU WANT!

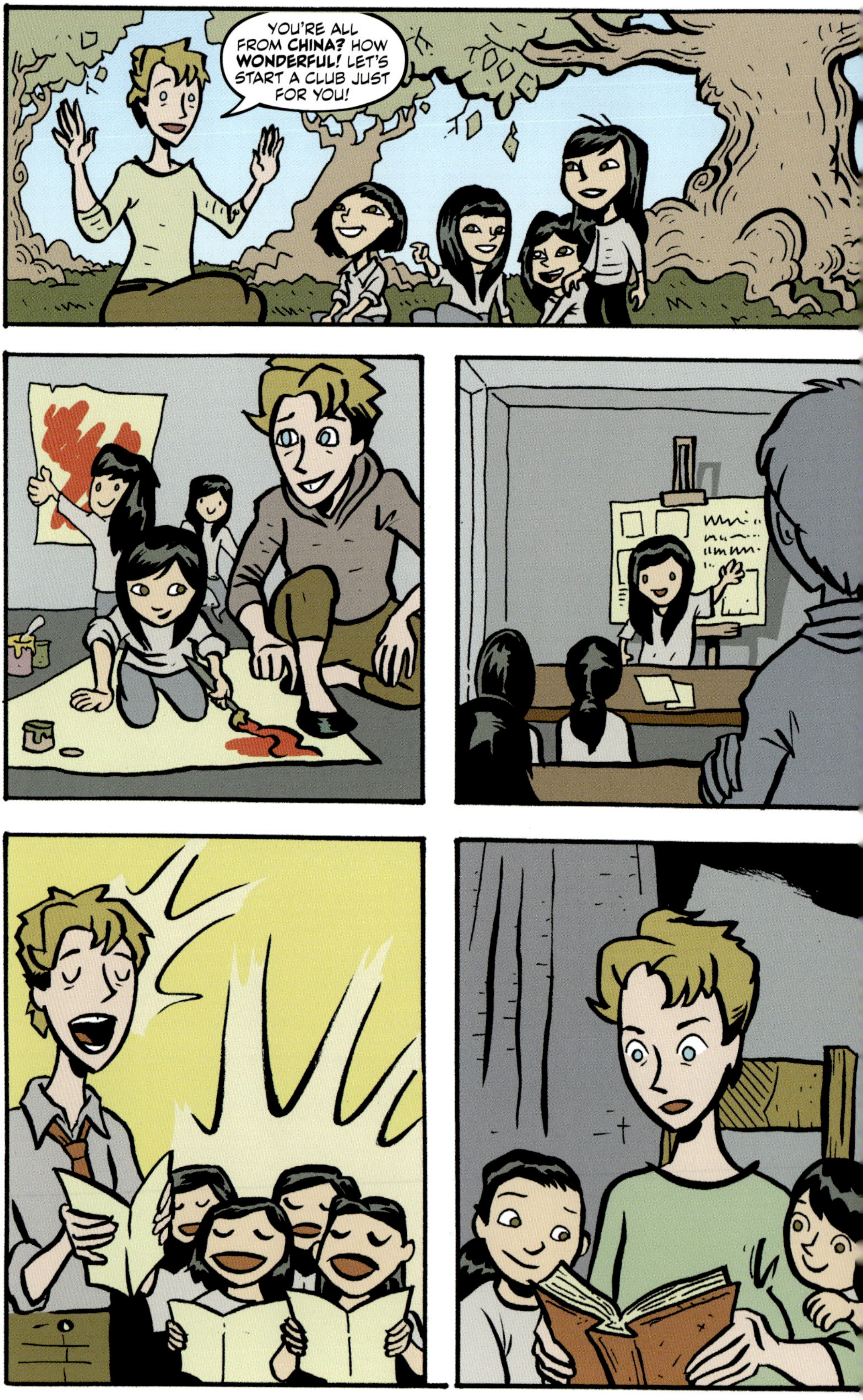
YOU'RE ALL FROM **CHINA?** HOW **WONDERFUL!** LET'S START A CLUB JUST FOR YOU!

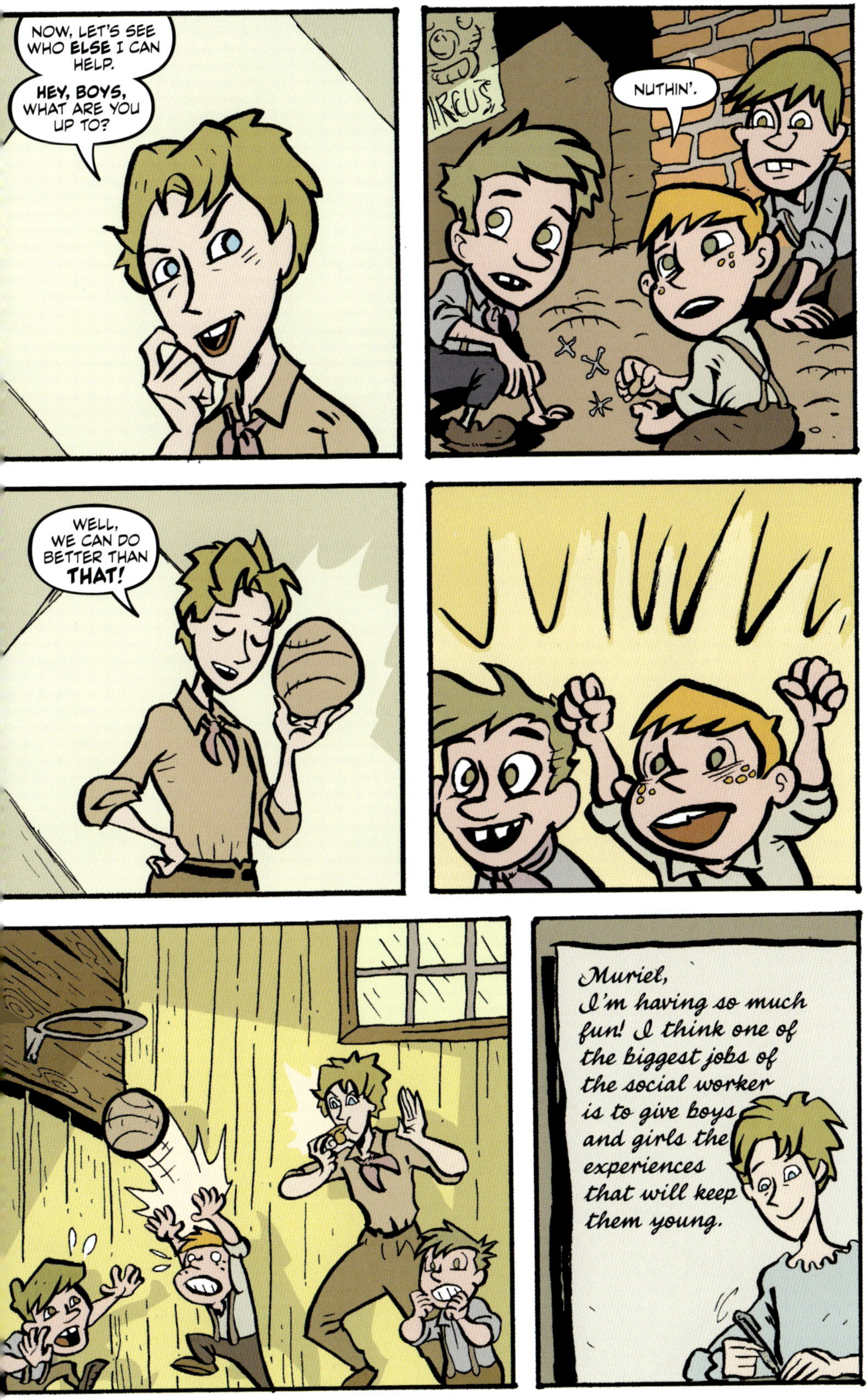
NOW, LET'S SEE WHO ELSE I CAN HELP.
HEY, BOYS, WHAT ARE YOU UP TO?
CIRCUS
NUTHIN'.
WELL, WE CAN DO BETTER THAN THAT!
Muriel,
I'm having so much fun! I think one of the biggest jobs of the social worker is to give boys and girls the experiences that will keep them young.

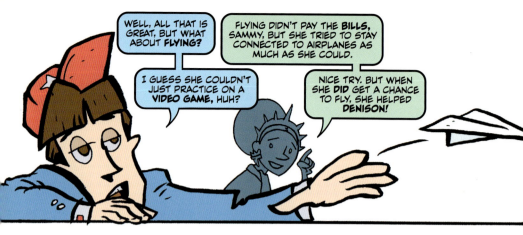

WELL, ALL THAT IS GREAT, BUT WHAT ABOUT **FLYING?**

FLYING DIDN'T PAY THE **BILLS,** SAMMY, BUT SHE TRIED TO STAY CONNECTED TO AIRPLANES AS MUCH AS SHE COULD.

I GUESS SHE COULDN'T JUST PRACTICE ON A **VIDEO GAME,** HUH?

NICE TRY. BUT WHEN SHE **DID** GET A CHANCE TO FLY, SHE HELPED **DENISON!**

SUPPORT DENISON HOUSE! HELP POOR CHILDREN HAVE BETTER LIVES!

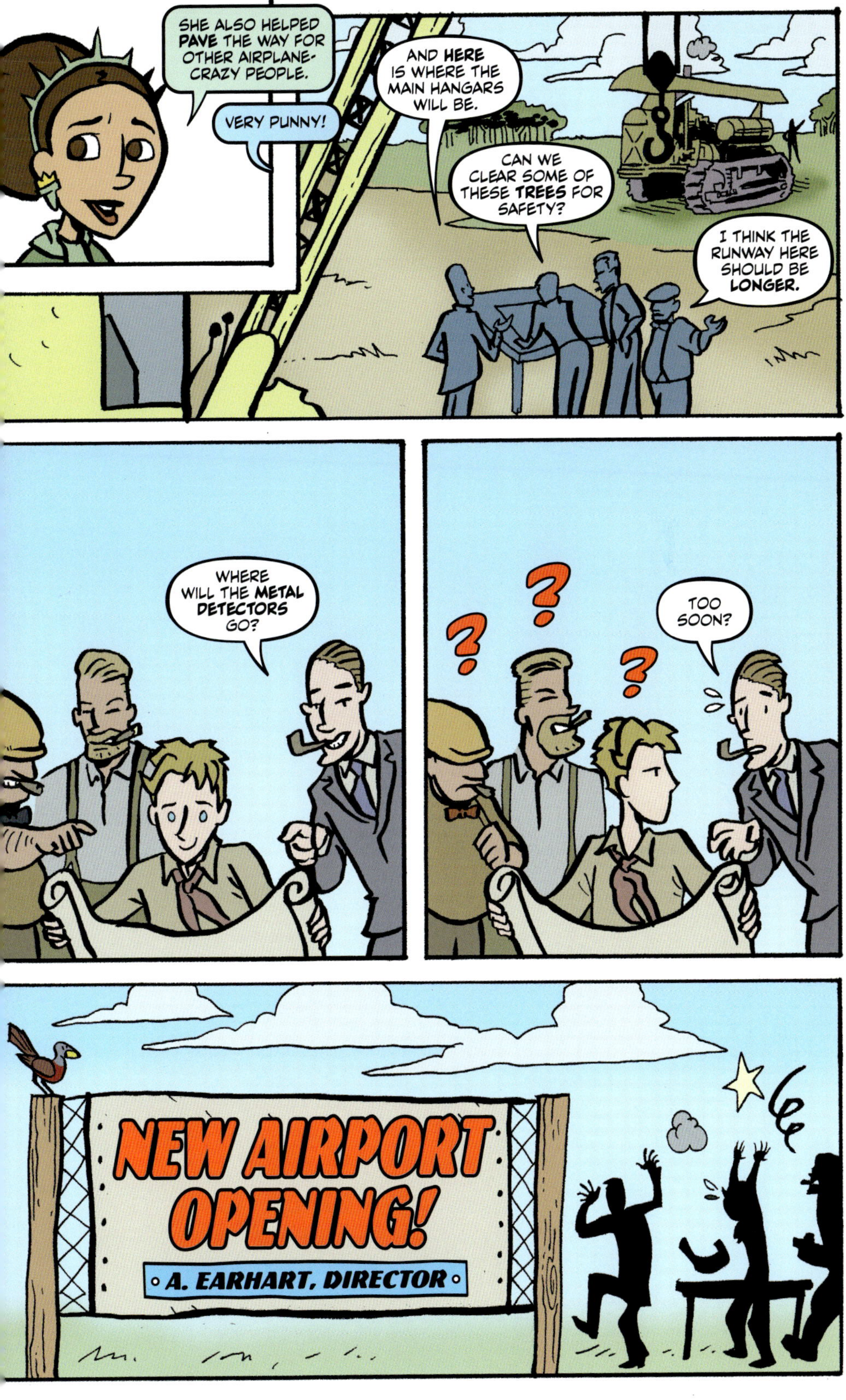
SHE ALSO HELPED PAVE THE WAY FOR OTHER AIRPLANE-CRAZY PEOPLE.
VERY PUNNY!
AND HERE IS WHERE THE MAIN HANGARS WILL BE.
CAN WE CLEAR SOME OF THESE TREES FOR SAFETY?
I THINK THE RUNWAY HERE SHOULD BE LONGER.
WHERE WILL THE METAL DETECTORS GO?
?
?
?
TOO SOON?
NEW AIRPORT OPENING!
A. EARHART, DIRECTOR

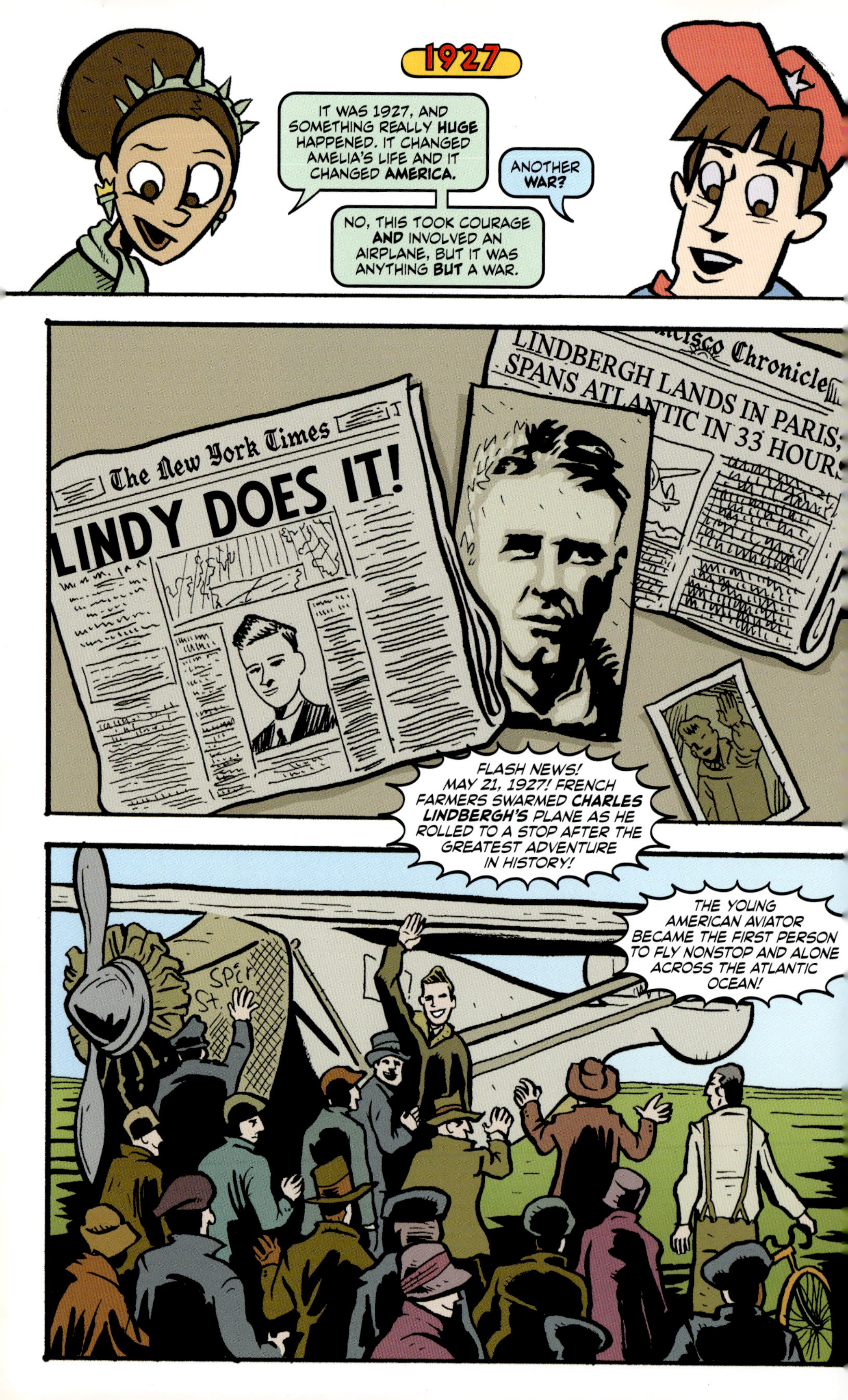
1927
IT WAS 1927, AND SOMETHING REALLY **HUGE** HAPPENED. IT CHANGED AMELIA'S LIFE AND IT CHANGED **AMERICA.**
ANOTHER **WAR?**
NO, THIS TOOK COURAGE **AND** INVOLVED AN AIRPLANE, BUT IT WAS ANYTHING **BUT** A WAR.
The New York Times
LINDY DOES IT!
LINDBERGH LANDS IN PARIS, SPANS ATLANTIC IN 33 HOURS
*FLASH NEWS! MAY 21, 1927! FRENCH FARMERS SWARMED **CHARLES LINDBERGH'S** PLANE AS HE ROLLED TO A STOP AFTER THE GREATEST ADVENTURE IN HISTORY!*
THE YOUNG AMERICAN AVIATOR BECAME THE FIRST PERSON TO FLY NONSTOP AND ALONE ACROSS THE ATLANTIC OCEAN!

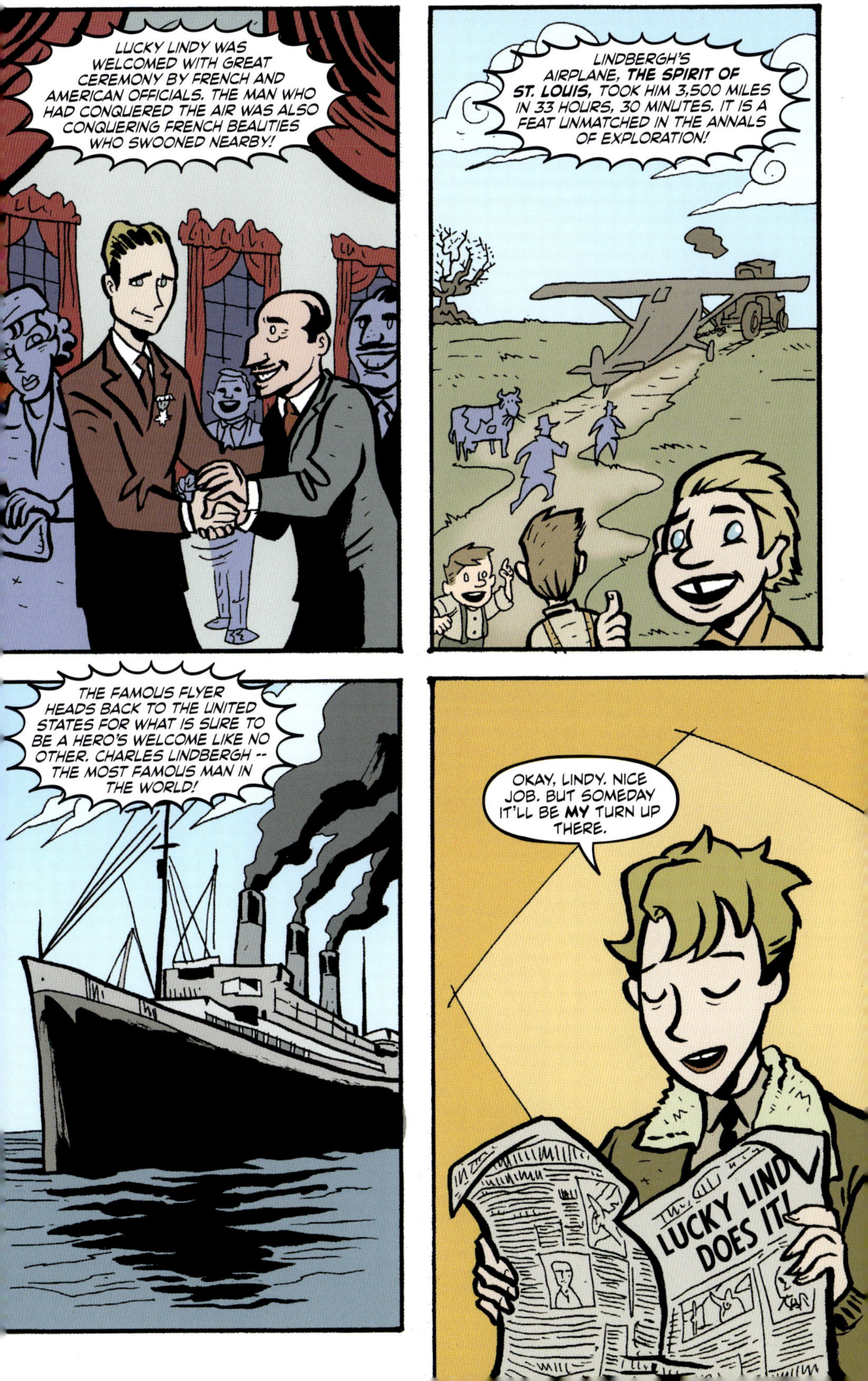
LUCKY LINDY WAS WELCOMED WITH GREAT CEREMONY BY FRENCH AND AMERICAN OFFICIALS. THE MAN WHO HAD CONQUERED THE AIR WAS ALSO CONQUERING FRENCH BEAUTIES WHO SWOONED NEARBY!
LINDBERGH'S AIRPLANE, **THE SPIRIT OF ST. LOUIS,** TOOK HIM 3,500 MILES IN 33 HOURS, 30 MINUTES. IT IS A FEAT UNMATCHED IN THE ANNALS OF EXPLORATION!
THE FAMOUS FLYER HEADS BACK TO THE UNITED STATES FOR WHAT IS SURE TO BE A HERO'S WELCOME LIKE NO OTHER. CHARLES LINDBERGH -- THE MOST FAMOUS MAN IN THE WORLD!
OKAY, LINDY. NICE JOB. BUT SOMEDAY IT'LL BE **MY** TURN UP THERE.
LUCKY LIND DOES IT!

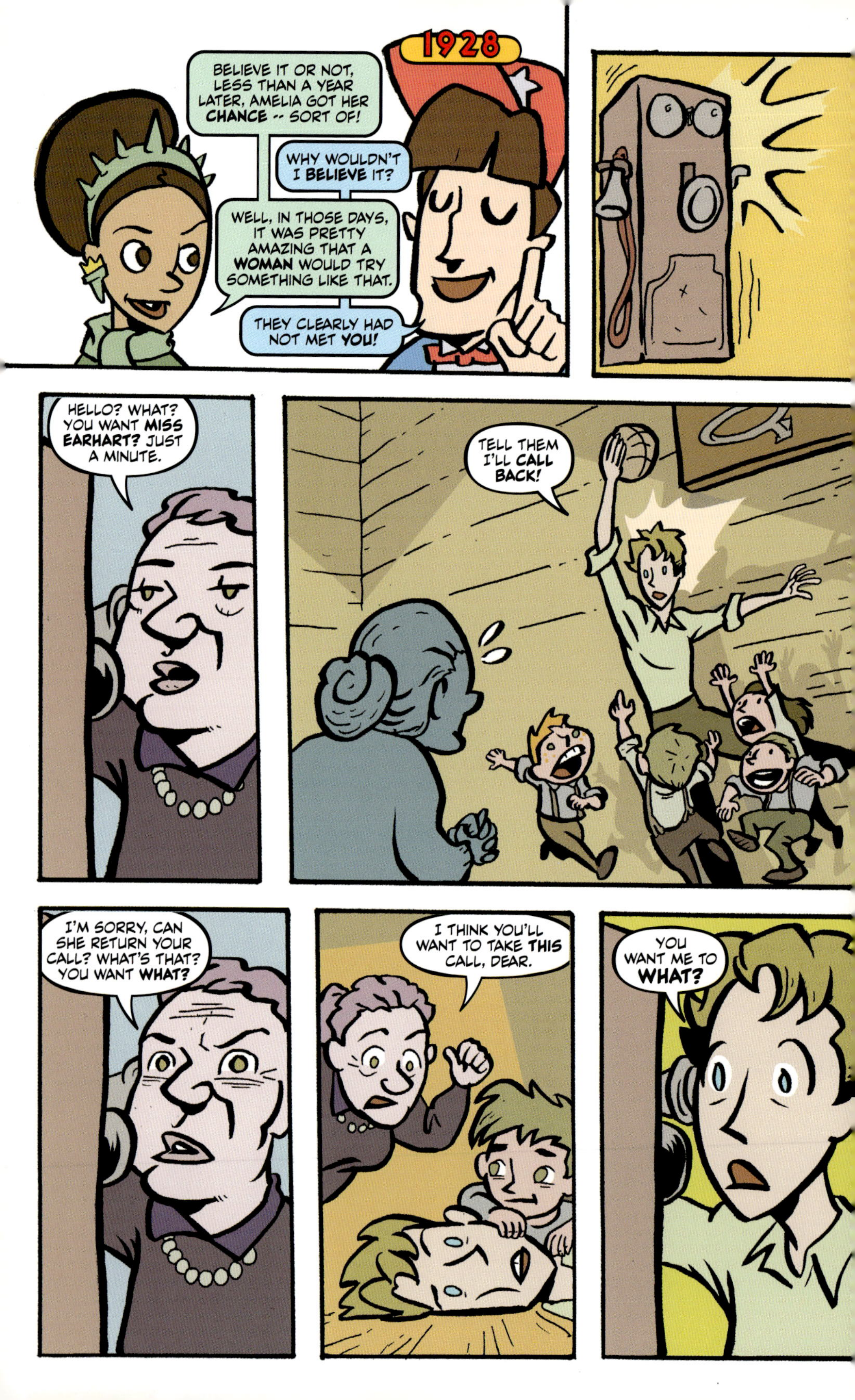
1928
BELIEVE IT OR NOT, LESS THAN A YEAR LATER, AMELIA GOT HER CHANCE -- SORT OF!
WHY WOULDN'T I BELIEVE IT?
WELL, IN THOSE DAYS, IT WAS PRETTY AMAZING THAT A WOMAN WOULD TRY SOMETHING LIKE THAT.
THEY CLEARLY HAD NOT MET YOU!
HELLO? WHAT? YOU WANT MISS EARHART? JUST A MINUTE.
TELL THEM I'LL CALL BACK!
I'M SORRY, CAN SHE RETURN YOUR CALL? WHAT'S THAT? YOU WANT WHAT?
I THINK YOU'LL WANT TO TAKE THIS CALL, DEAR.
YOU WANT ME TO WHAT?

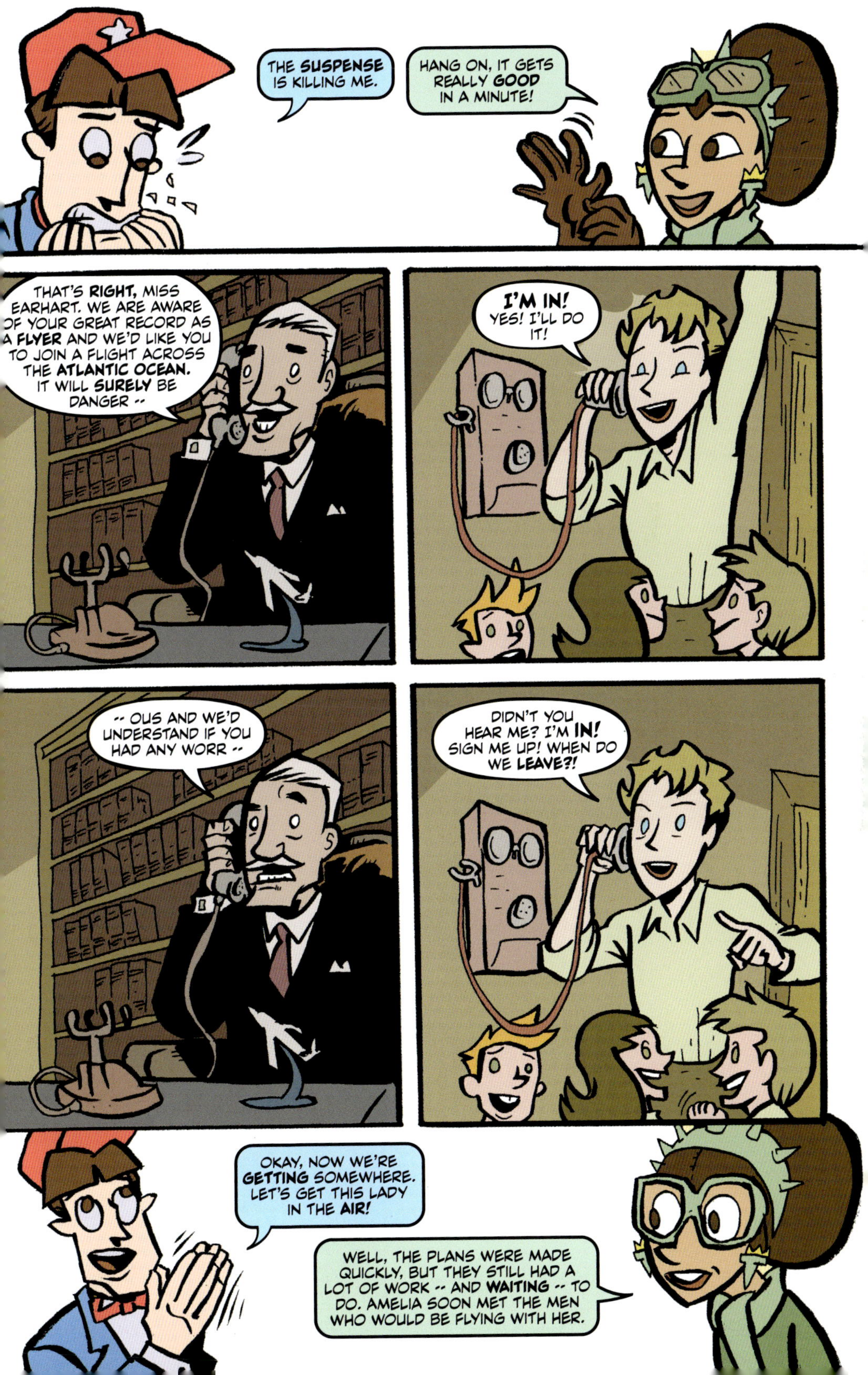
THE SUSPENSE IS KILLING ME.
HANG ON, IT GETS REALLY GOOD IN A MINUTE!
THAT'S RIGHT, MISS EARHART. WE ARE AWARE OF YOUR GREAT RECORD AS A FLYER AND WE'D LIKE YOU TO JOIN A FLIGHT ACROSS THE ATLANTIC OCEAN. IT WILL SURELY BE DANGER --
I'M IN! YES! I'LL DO IT!
-- OUS AND WE'D UNDERSTAND IF YOU HAD ANY WORR --
DIDN'T YOU HEAR ME? I'M IN! SIGN ME UP! WHEN DO WE LEAVE?!
OKAY, NOW WE'RE GETTING SOMEWHERE. LET'S GET THIS LADY IN THE AIR!
WELL, THE PLANS WERE MADE QUICKLY, BUT THEY STILL HAD A LOT OF WORK -- AND WAITING -- TO DO. AMELIA SOON MET THE MEN WHO WOULD BE FLYING WITH HER.

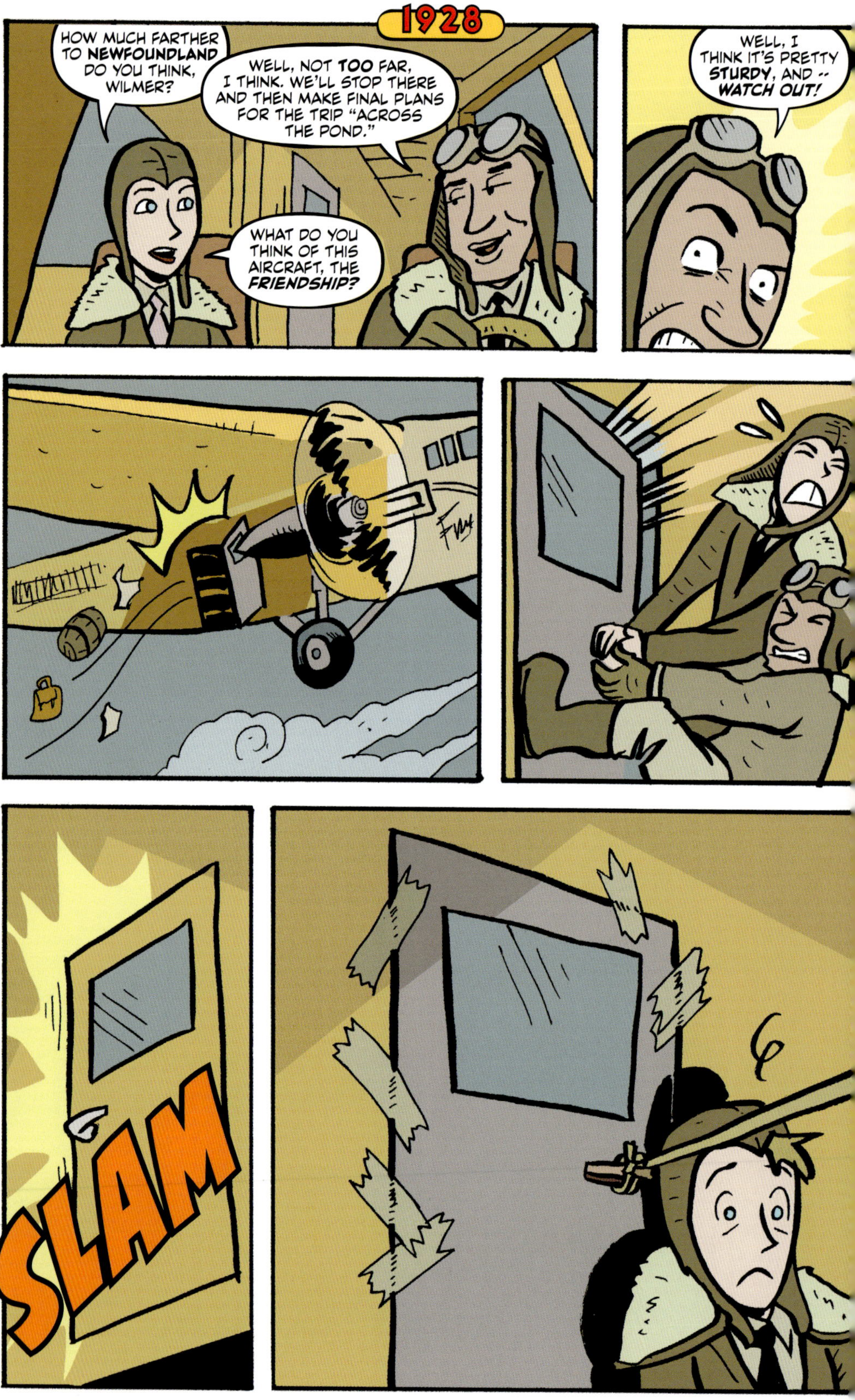
1928
HOW MUCH FARTHER TO NEWFOUNDLAND DO YOU THINK, WILMER?
WELL, NOT TOO FAR, I THINK. WE'LL STOP THERE AND THEN MAKE FINAL PLANS FOR THE TRIP "ACROSS THE POND."
WHAT DO YOU THINK OF THIS AIRCRAFT, THE FRIENDSHIP?
WELL, I THINK IT'S PRETTY STURDY, AND -- WATCH OUT!
SLAM

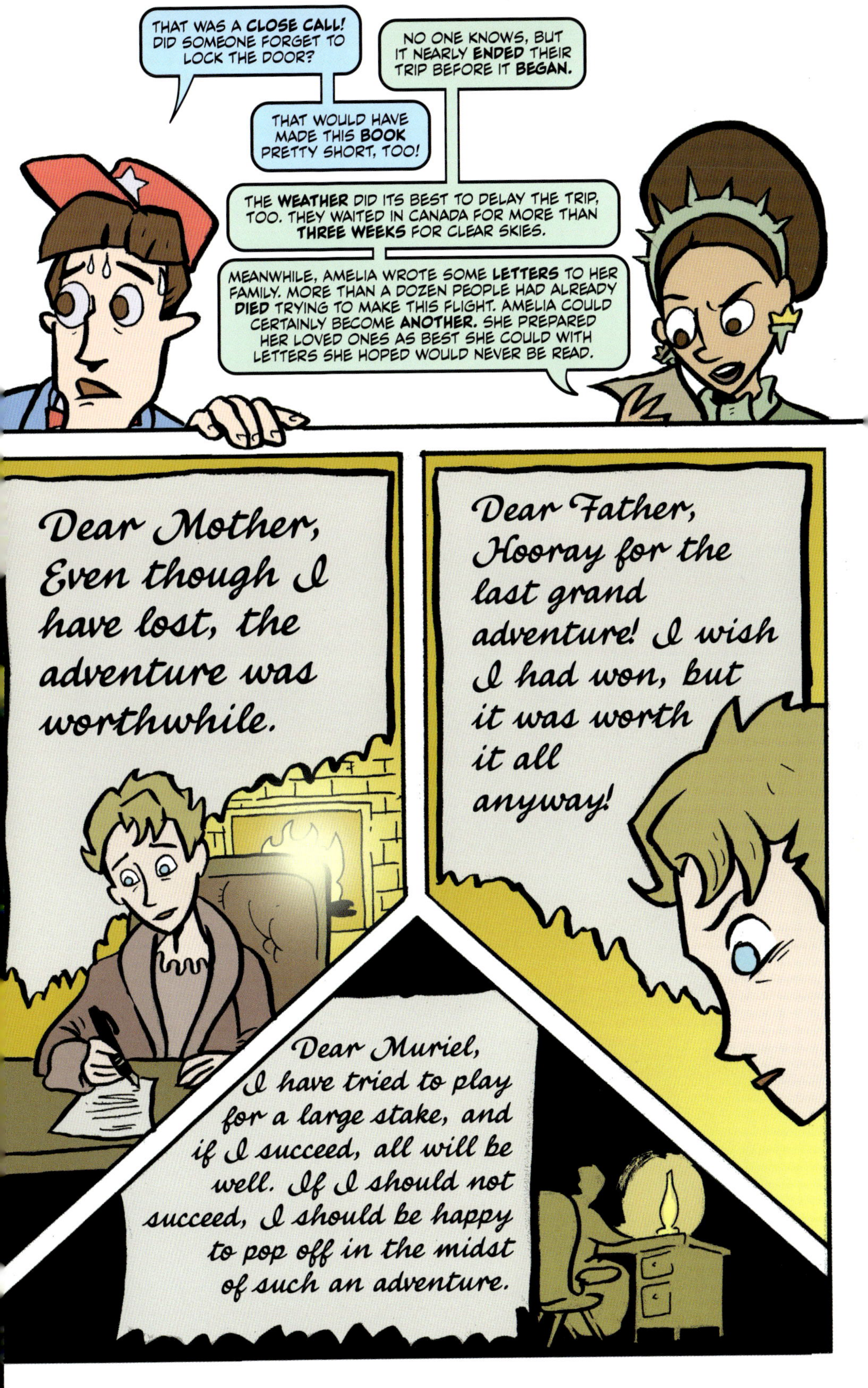
THAT WAS A CLOSE CALL! DID SOMEONE FORGET TO LOCK THE DOOR?
NO ONE KNOWS, BUT IT NEARLY ENDED THEIR TRIP BEFORE IT BEGAN.
THAT WOULD HAVE MADE THIS BOOK PRETTY SHORT, TOO!
THE WEATHER DID ITS BEST TO DELAY THE TRIP, TOO. THEY WAITED IN CANADA FOR MORE THAN THREE WEEKS FOR CLEAR SKIES.
MEANWHILE, AMELIA WROTE SOME LETTERS TO HER FAMILY. MORE THAN A DOZEN PEOPLE HAD ALREADY DIED TRYING TO MAKE THIS FLIGHT. AMELIA COULD CERTAINLY BECOME ANOTHER. SHE PREPARED HER LOVED ONES AS BEST SHE COULD WITH LETTERS SHE HOPED WOULD NEVER BE READ.
Dear Mother, Even though I have lost, the adventure was worthwhile.
Dear Father, Hooray for the last grand adventure! I wish I had won, but it was worth it all anyway!
Dear Muriel, I have tried to play for a large stake, and if I succeed, all will be well. If I should not succeed, I should be happy to pop off in the midst of such an adventure.

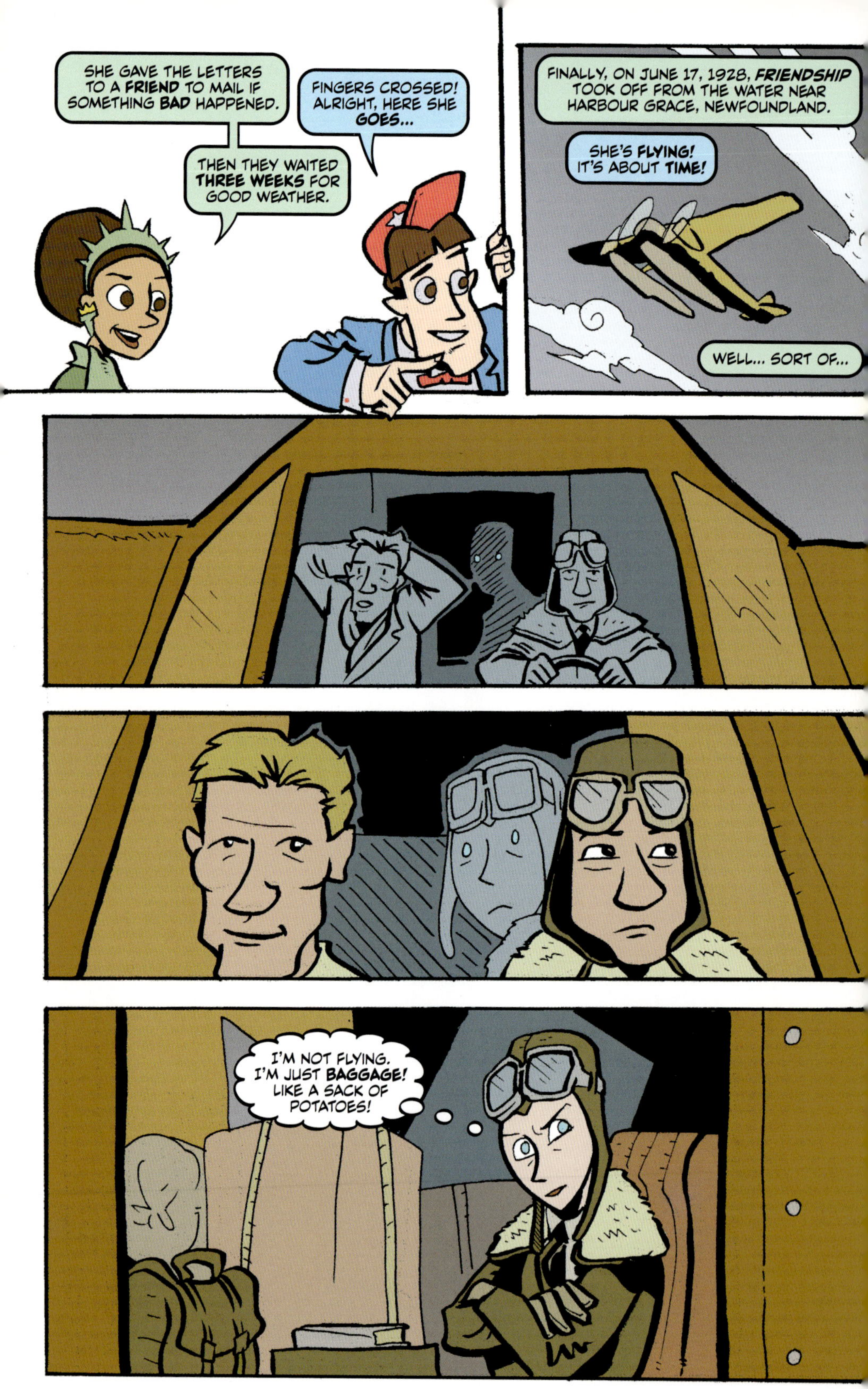
SHE GAVE THE LETTERS TO A FRIEND TO MAIL IF SOMETHING BAD HAPPENED.
THEN THEY WAITED THREE WEEKS FOR GOOD WEATHER.
FINGERS CROSSED! ALRIGHT, HERE SHE GOES...
FINALLY, ON JUNE 17, 1928, FRIENDSHIP TOOK OFF FROM THE WATER NEAR HARBOUR GRACE, NEWFOUNDLAND.
SHE'S FLYING! IT'S ABOUT TIME!
WELL... SORT OF...
I'M NOT FLYING. I'M JUST BAGGAGE! LIKE A SACK OF POTATOES!

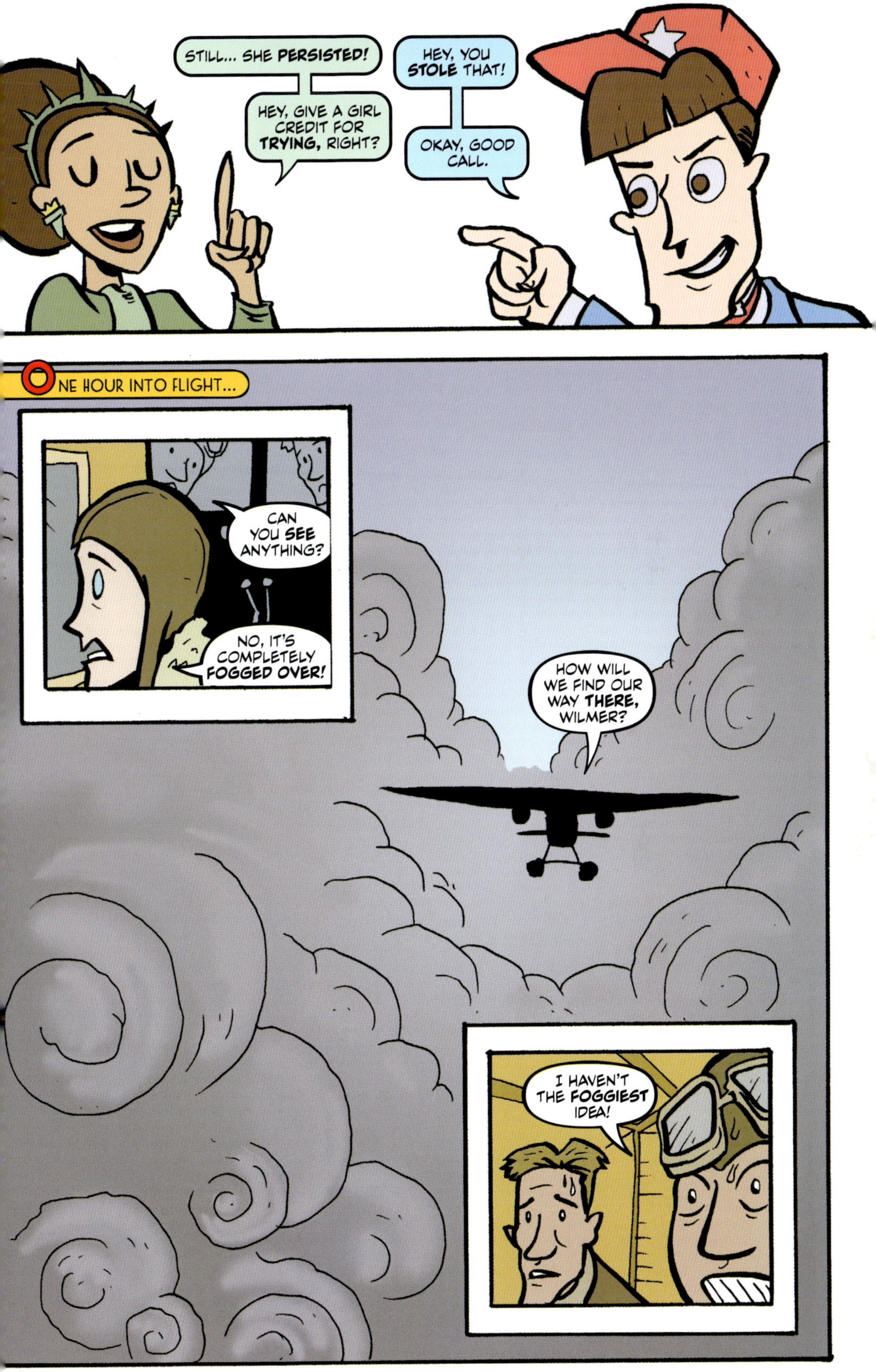
STILL... SHE PERSISTED!
HEY, GIVE A GIRL CREDIT FOR TRYING, RIGHT?
HEY, YOU STOLE THAT!
OKAY, GOOD CALL.
ONE HOUR INTO FLIGHT...
CAN YOU SEE ANYTHING?
NO, IT'S COMPLETELY FOGGED OVER!
HOW WILL WE FIND OUR WAY THERE, WILMER?
I HAVEN'T THE FOGGIEST IDEA!

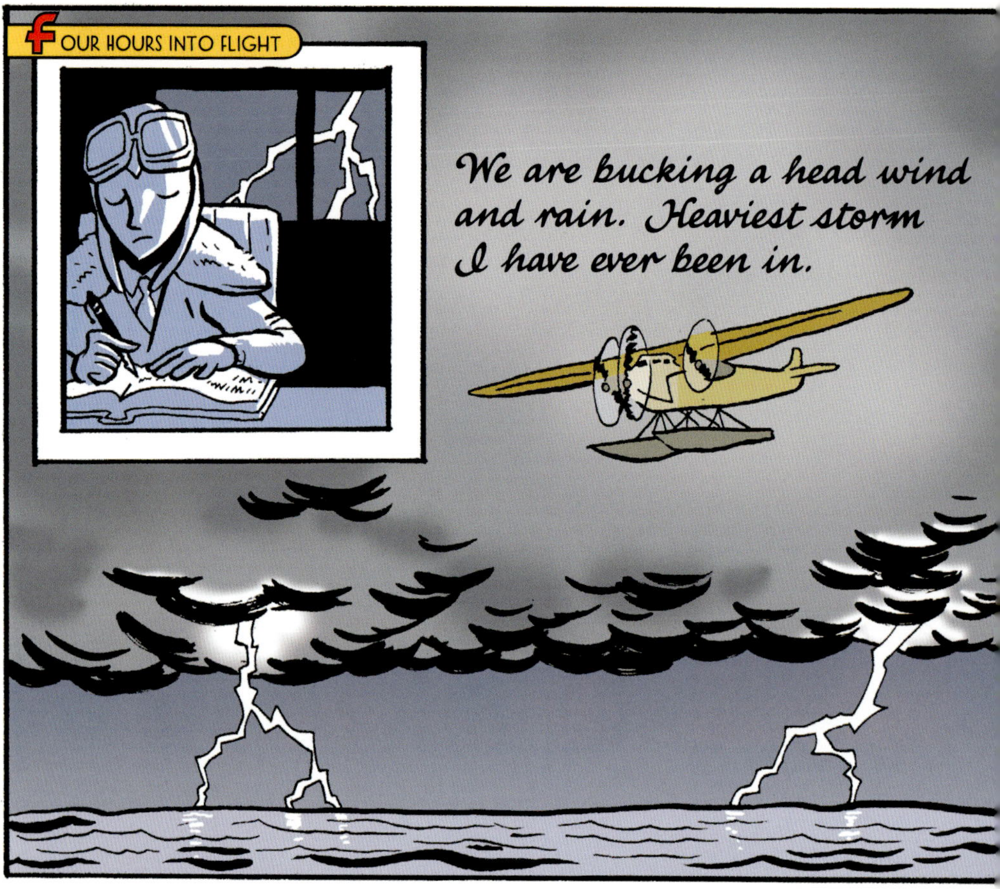
FOUR HOURS INTO FLIGHT
We are bucking a head wind and rain. Heaviest storm I have ever been in.

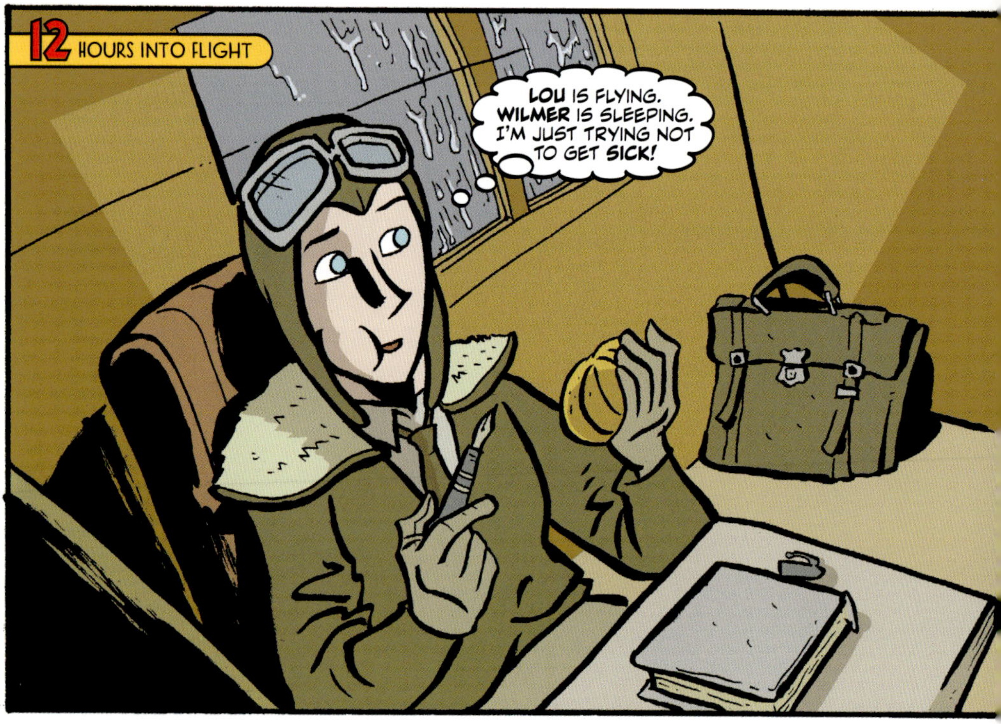
12 HOURS INTO FLIGHT
LOU IS FLYING. WILMER IS SLEEPING. I'M JUST TRYING NOT TO GET SICK!

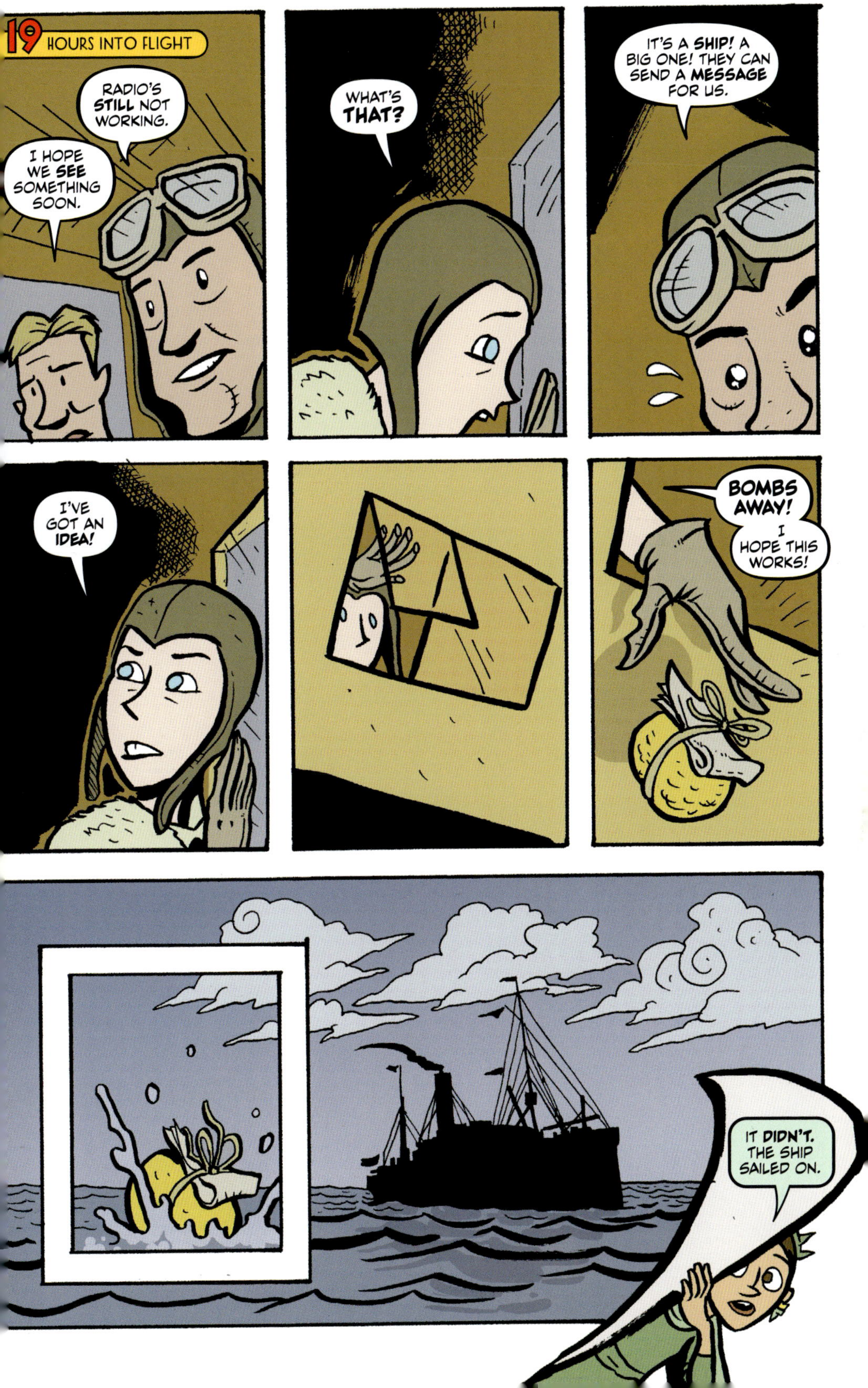
19 HOURS INTO FLIGHT
RADIO'S STILL NOT WORKING.
I HOPE WE SEE SOMETHING SOON.
WHAT'S THAT?
IT'S A SHIP! A BIG ONE! THEY CAN SEND A MESSAGE FOR US.
I'VE GOT AN IDEA!
BOMBS AWAY!
I HOPE THIS WORKS!
IT DIDN'T. THE SHIP SAILED ON.

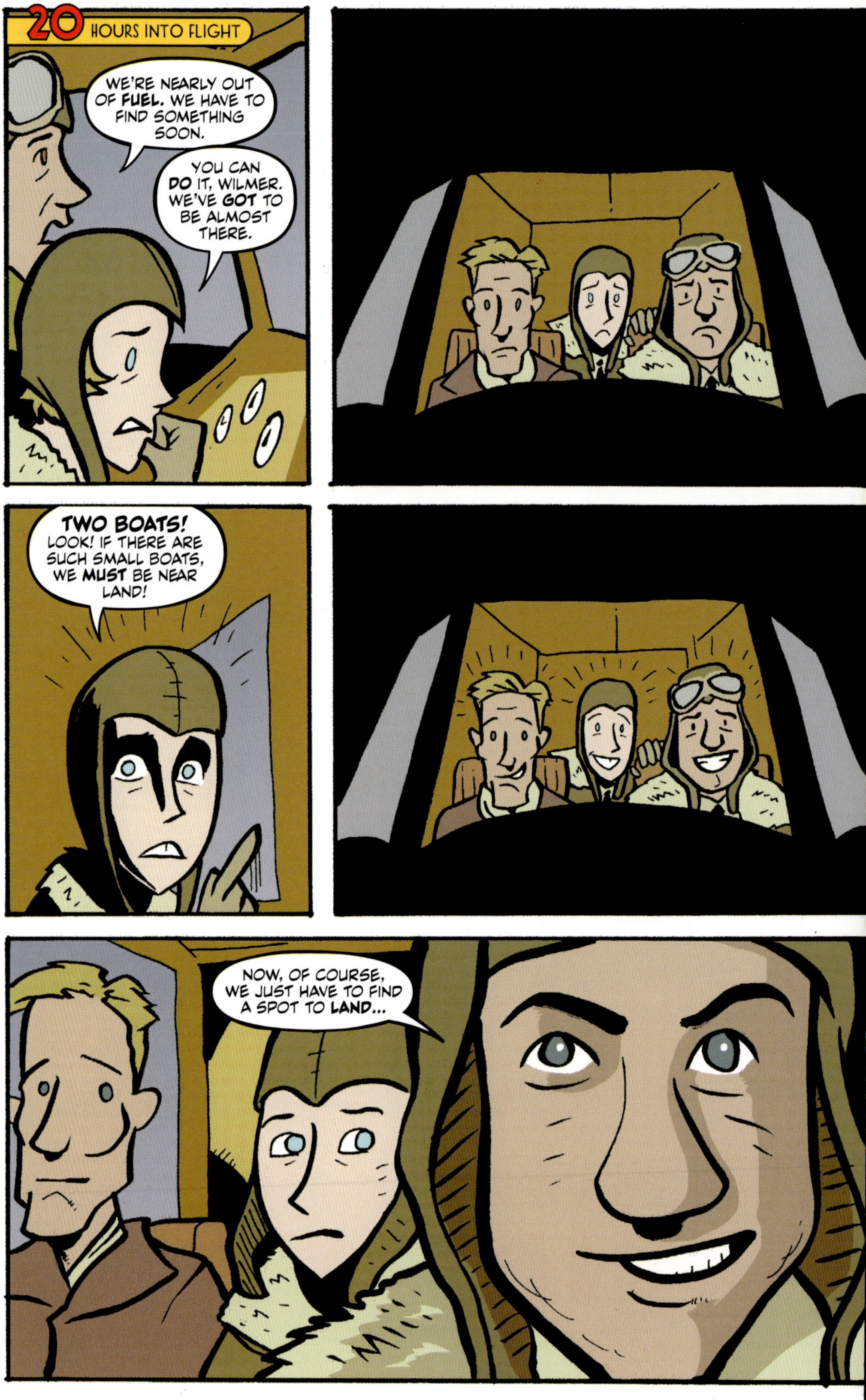
20 HOURS INTO FLIGHT
WE'RE NEARLY OUT OF FUEL. WE HAVE TO FIND SOMETHING SOON.
YOU CAN DO IT, WILMER. WE'VE GOT TO BE ALMOST THERE.
TWO BOATS! LOOK! IF THERE ARE SUCH SMALL BOATS, WE MUST BE NEAR LAND!
NOW, OF COURSE, WE JUST HAVE TO FIND A SPOT TO LAND...

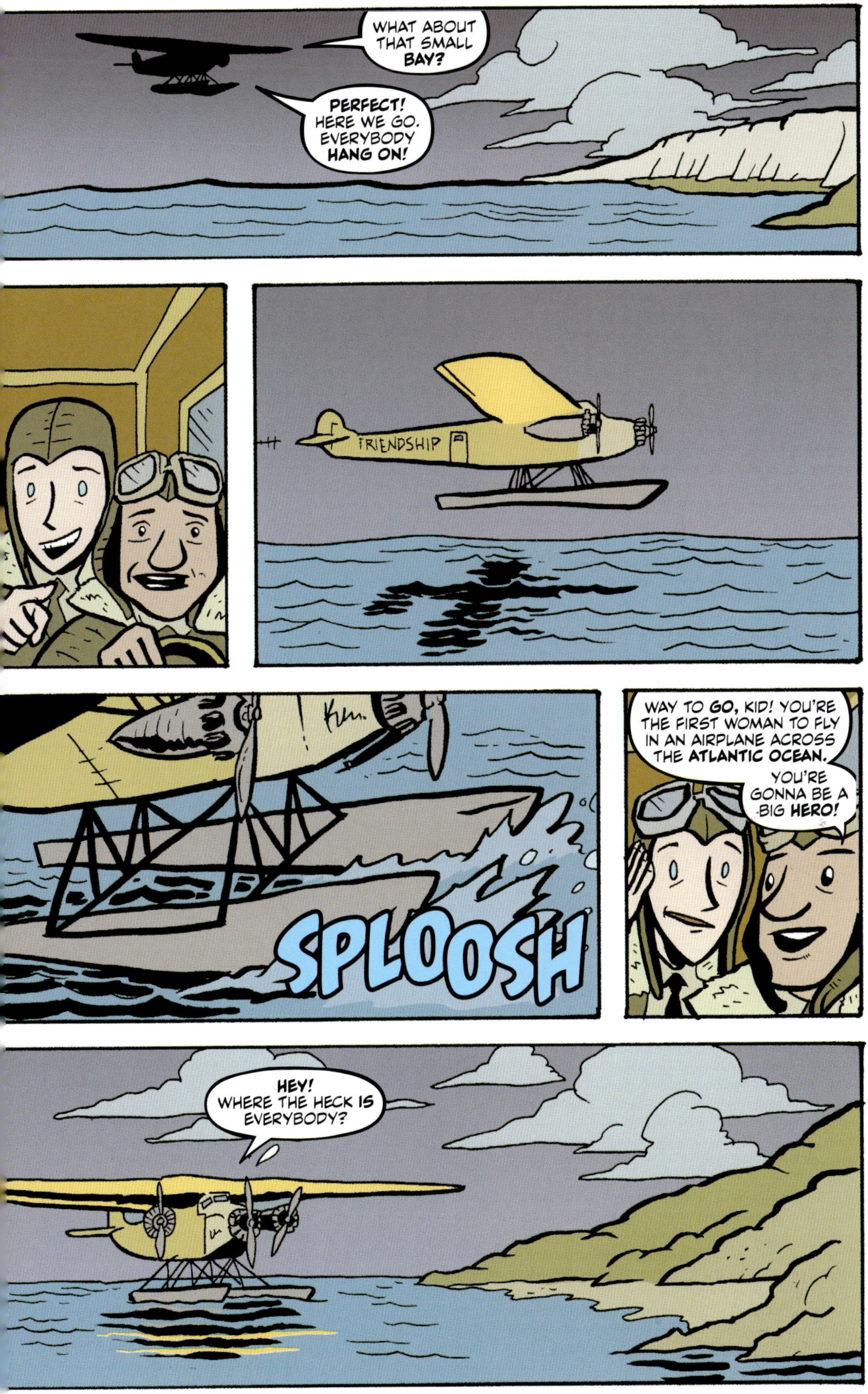
WHAT ABOUT THAT SMALL BAY?
PERFECT! HERE WE GO. EVERYBODY HANG ON!
FRIENDSHIP
SPLOOSH
WAY TO GO, KID! YOU'RE THE FIRST WOMAN TO FLY IN AN AIRPLANE ACROSS THE ATLANTIC OCEAN.
YOU'RE GONNA BE A BIG HERO!
HEY! WHERE THE HECK IS EVERYBODY?

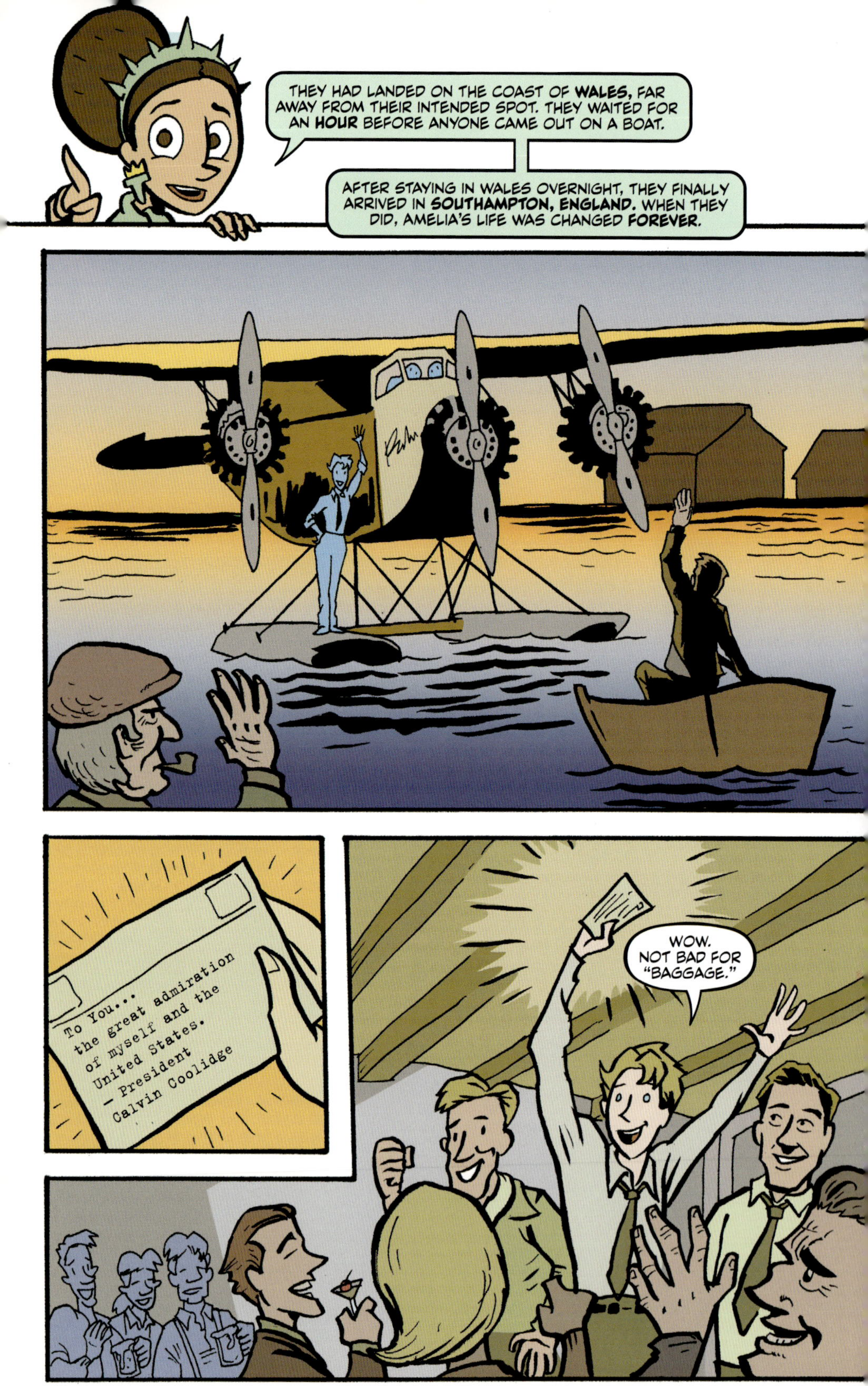
THEY HAD LANDED ON THE COAST OF **WALES,** FAR AWAY FROM THEIR INTENDED SPOT. THEY WAITED FOR AN **HOUR** BEFORE ANYONE CAME OUT ON A BOAT.
AFTER STAYING IN WALES OVERNIGHT, THEY FINALLY ARRIVED IN **SOUTHAMPTON, ENGLAND.** WHEN THEY DID, AMELIA'S LIFE WAS CHANGED **FOREVER.**
To You... the great admiration of myself and the United States. - President Calvin Coolidge
WOW. NOT BAD FOR "BAGGAGE."

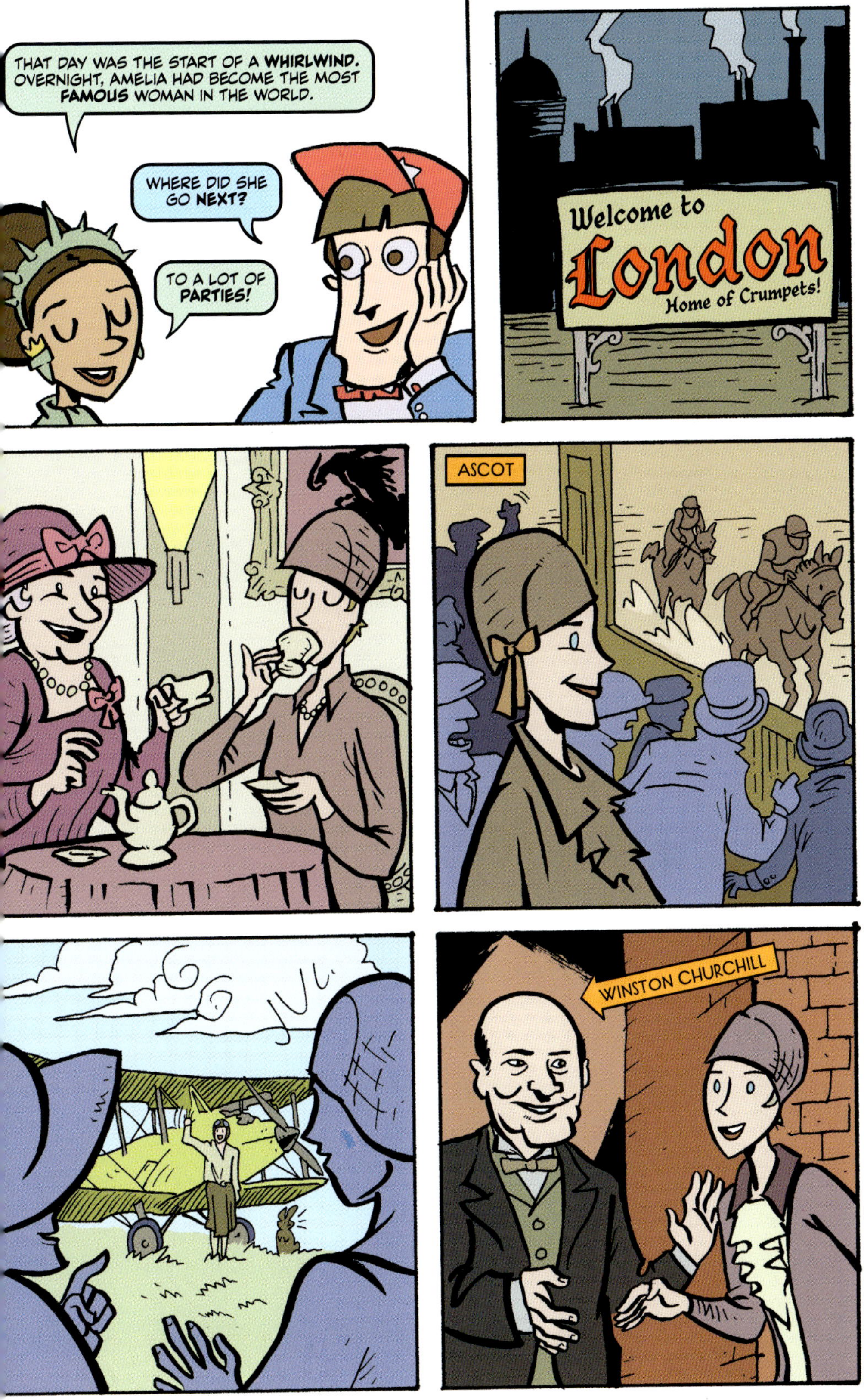
THAT DAY WAS THE START OF A **WHIRLWIND.** OVERNIGHT, AMELIA HAD BECOME THE MOST **FAMOUS** WOMAN IN THE WORLD.
WHERE DID SHE GO **NEXT?**
TO A LOT OF **PARTIES!**
Welcome to London Home of Crumpets!
ASCOT
WINSTON CHURCHILL

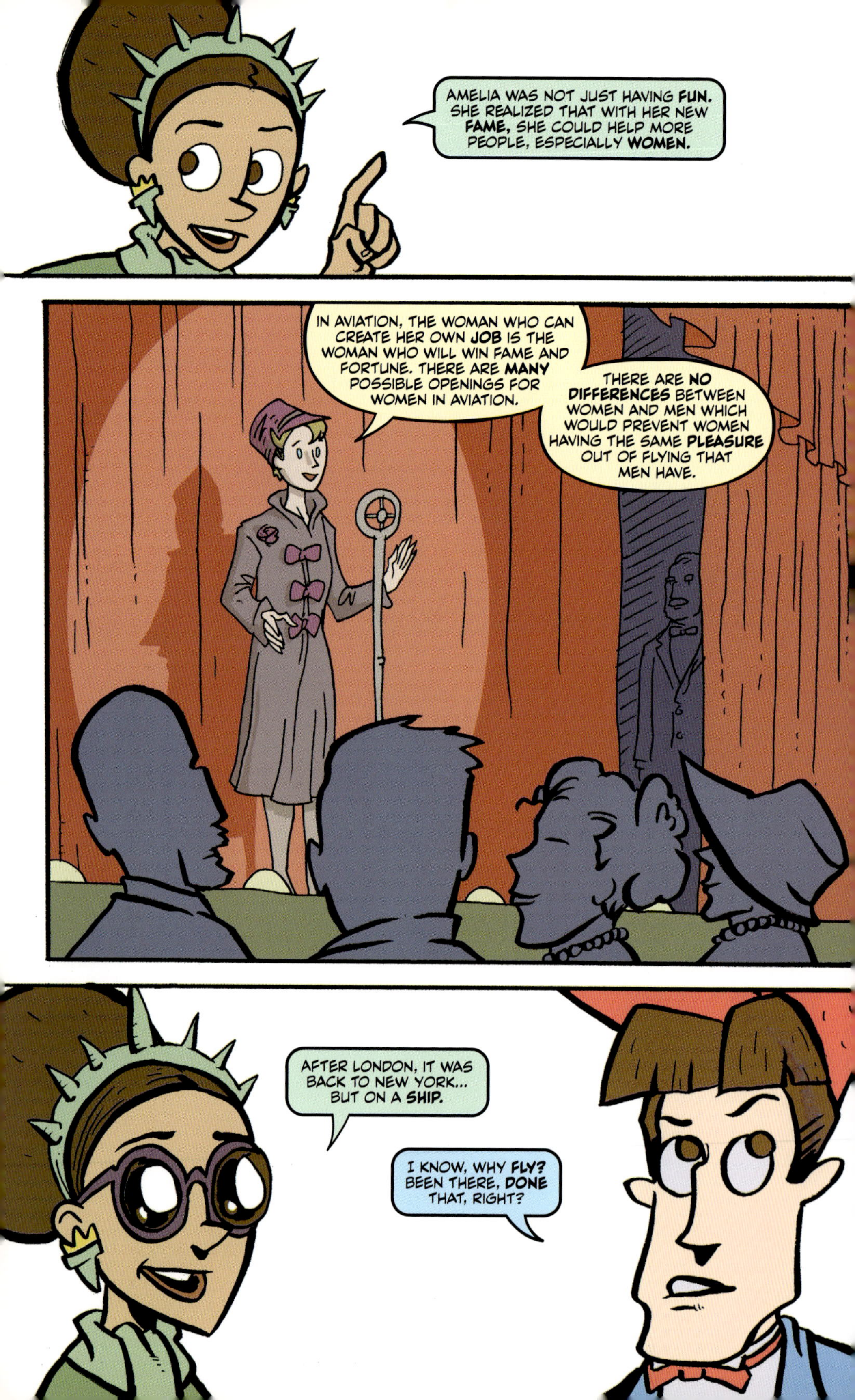
AMELIA WAS NOT JUST HAVING **FUN.** SHE REALIZED THAT WITH HER NEW **FAME,** SHE COULD HELP MORE PEOPLE, ESPECIALLY **WOMEN.**
IN AVIATION, THE WOMAN WHO CAN CREATE HER OWN **JOB** IS THE WOMAN WHO WILL WIN FAME AND FORTUNE. THERE ARE **MANY** POSSIBLE OPENINGS FOR WOMEN IN AVIATION.
THERE ARE **NO DIFFERENCES** BETWEEN WOMEN AND MEN WHICH WOULD PREVENT WOMEN HAVING THE SAME **PLEASURE** OUT OF FLYING THAT MEN HAVE.
AFTER LONDON, IT WAS BACK TO NEW YORK... BUT ON A **SHIP.**
I KNOW, WHY **FLY?** BEEN THERE, **DONE** THAT, RIGHT?

WELCOME TO
NEW YORK CITY
Home of the
Statue of Liberty!

HEY, **THAT** SOUNDS FAMILIAR.

GEE... I WONDER **WHY?**

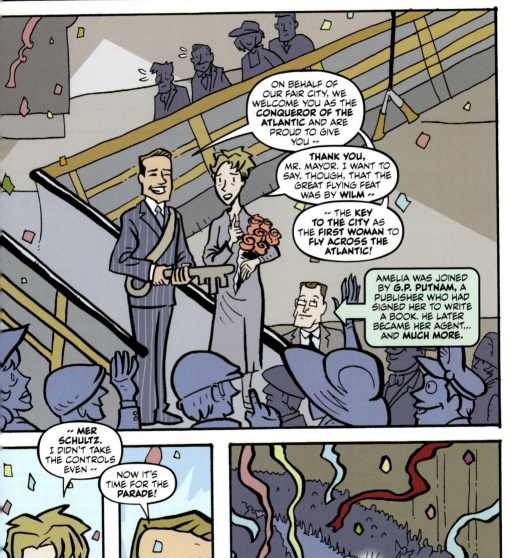

ON BEHALF OF OUR FAIR CITY, WE WELCOME YOU AS THE **CONQUEROR OF THE ATLANTIC** AND ARE PROUD TO GIVE YOU --

THANK YOU, MR. MAYOR. I WANT TO SAY, THOUGH, THAT THE GREAT FLYING FEAT WAS BY **WILM** --

-- THE **KEY TO THE CITY** AS THE **FIRST WOMAN** TO FLY ACROSS THE **ATLANTIC!**

AMELIA WAS JOINED BY **G.P. PUTNAM,** A PUBLISHER WHO HAD SIGNED HER TO WRITE A BOOK. HE LATER BECAME HER AGENT... AND **MUCH MORE.**

-- MER **SCHULTZ.** I DIDN'T TAKE THE CONTROLS EVEN --

NOW IT'S TIME FOR THE **PARADE!**

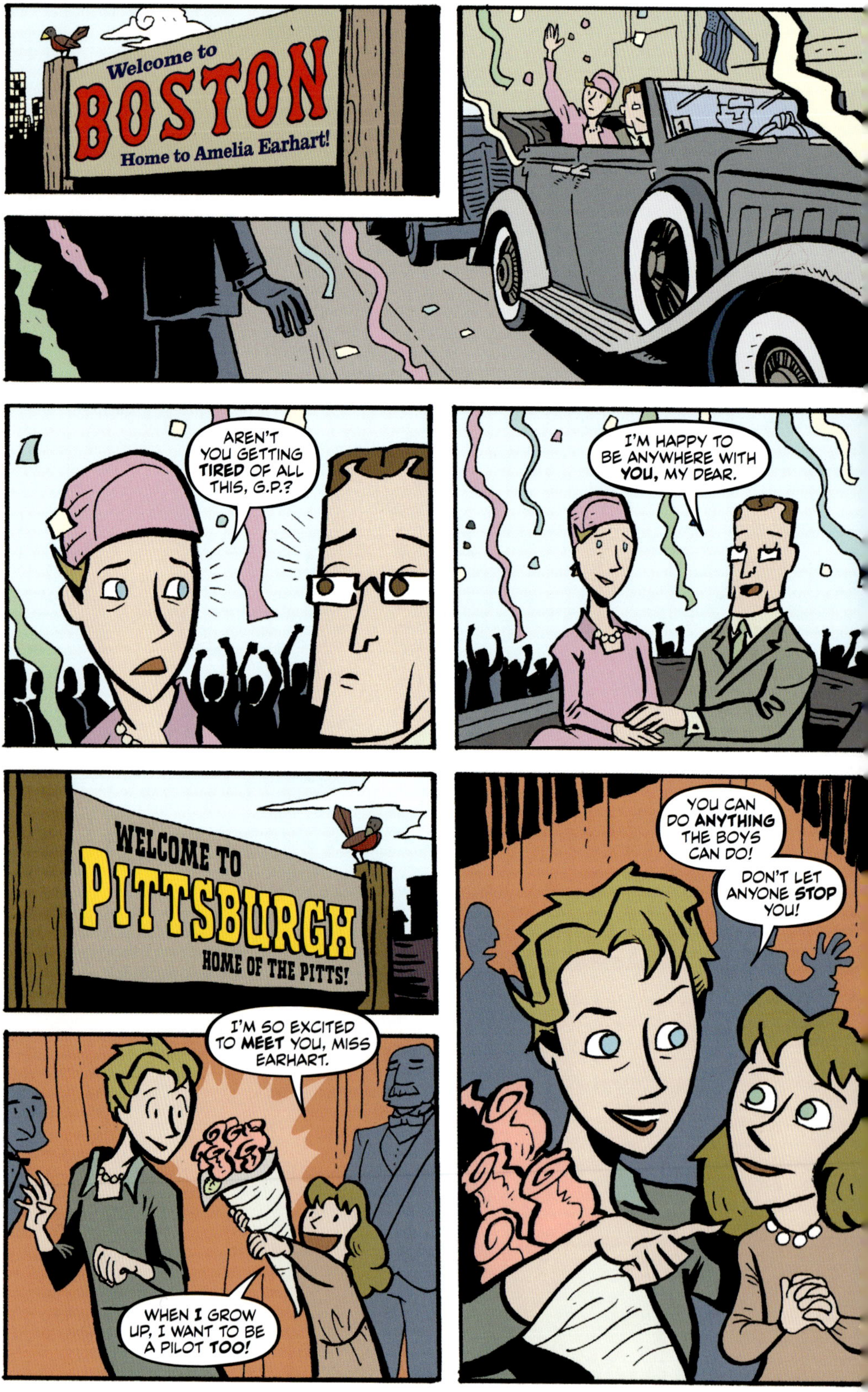
Welcome to
BOSTON
Home to Amelia Earhart!
AREN'T YOU GETTING TIRED OF ALL THIS, G.P.?
I'M HAPPY TO BE ANYWHERE WITH YOU, MY DEAR.
WELCOME TO
PITTSBURGH
HOME OF THE PITTS!
I'M SO EXCITED TO MEET YOU, MISS EARHART.
WHEN I GROW UP, I WANT TO BE A PILOT TOO!
YOU CAN DO ANYTHING THE BOYS CAN DO!
DON'T LET ANYONE STOP YOU!

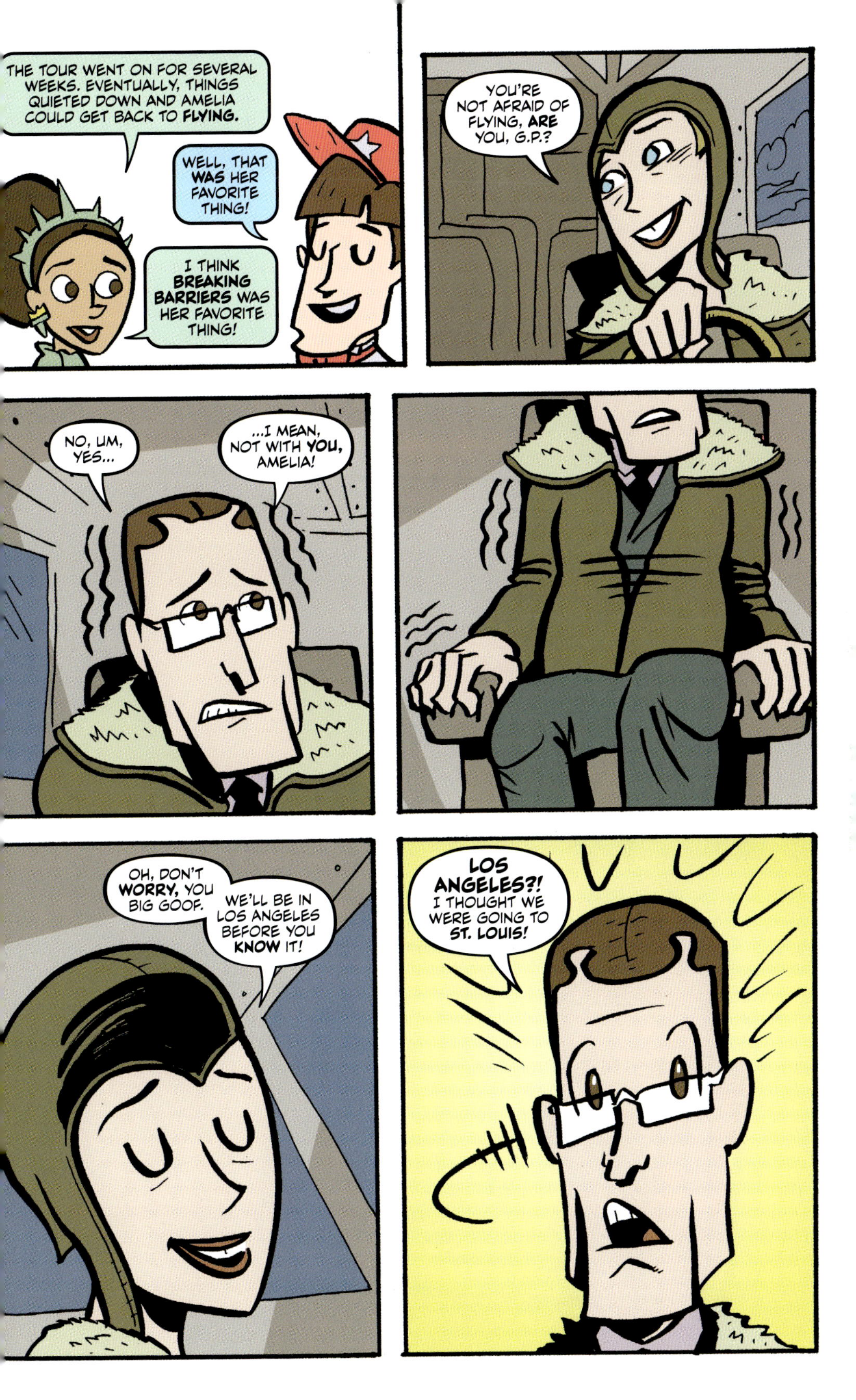
THE TOUR WENT ON FOR SEVERAL WEEKS. EVENTUALLY, THINGS QUIETED DOWN AND AMELIA COULD GET BACK TO **FLYING.**
WELL, THAT **WAS** HER FAVORITE THING!
I THINK **BREAKING BARRIERS** WAS HER FAVORITE THING!
YOU'RE NOT AFRAID OF FLYING, **ARE** YOU, G.P.?
NO, UM, YES...
...I MEAN, NOT WITH **YOU,** AMELIA!
OH, DON'T **WORRY,** YOU BIG GOOF.
WE'LL BE IN LOS ANGELES BEFORE YOU **KNOW** IT!
LOS ANGELES?! I THOUGHT WE WERE GOING TO **ST. LOUIS!**

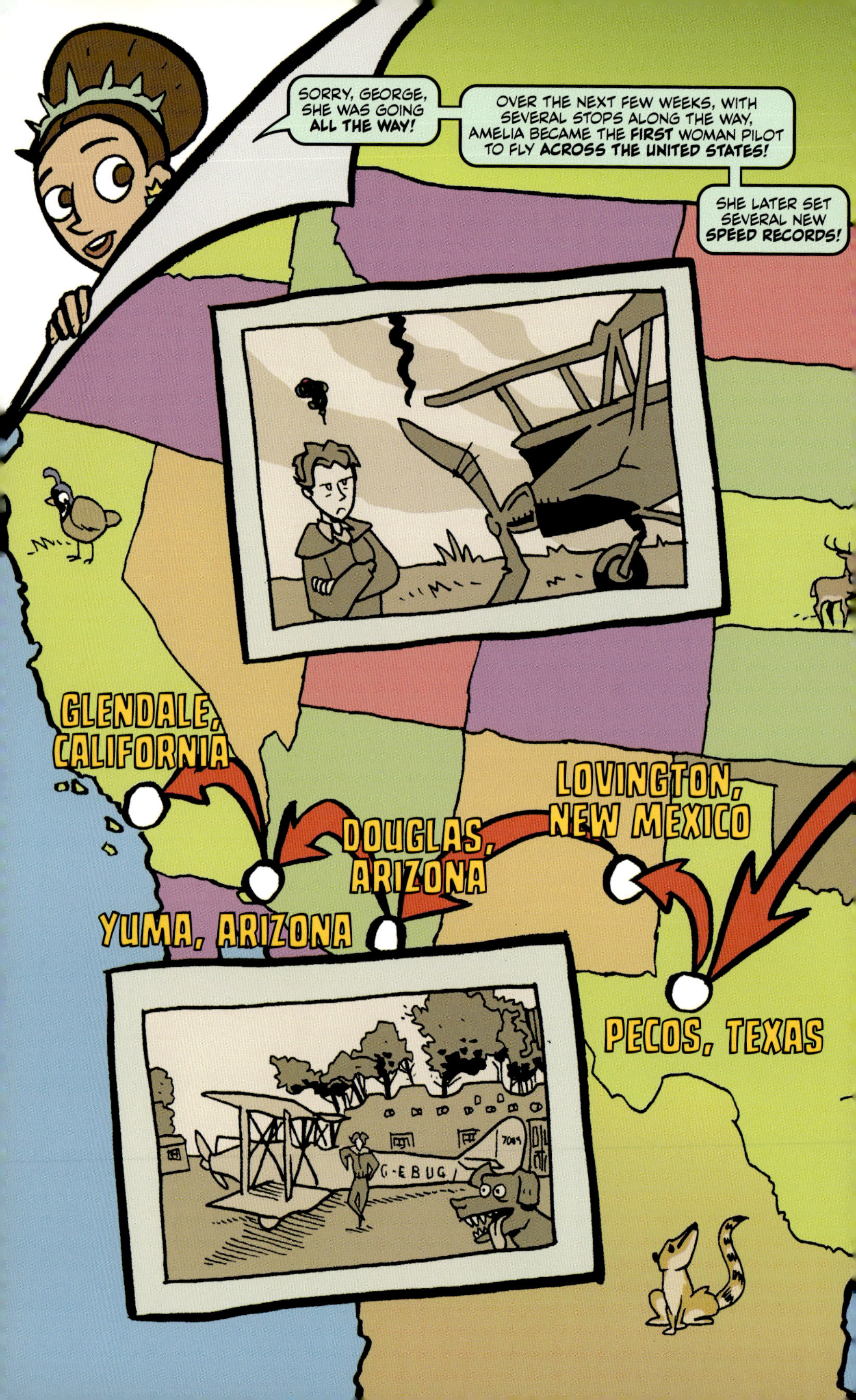
SORRY, GEORGE, SHE WAS GOING ALL THE WAY!
OVER THE NEXT FEW WEEKS, WITH SEVERAL STOPS ALONG THE WAY, AMELIA BECAME THE FIRST WOMAN PILOT TO FLY ACROSS THE UNITED STATES!
SHE LATER SET SEVERAL NEW SPEED RECORDS!
GLENDALE, CALIFORNIA
LOVINGTON, NEW MEXICO
DOUGLAS, ARIZONA
YUMA, ARIZONA
PECOS, TEXAS
G-EBUG

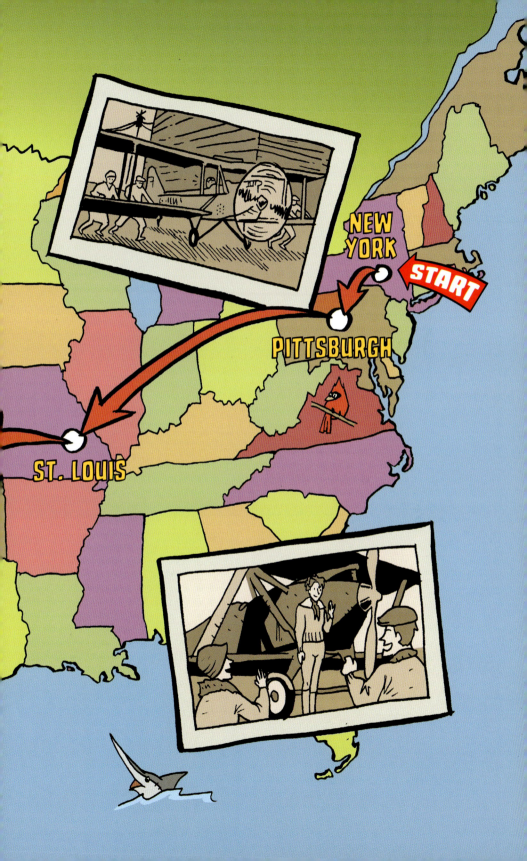

NEW YORK

START

PITTSBURGH

ST. LOUIS

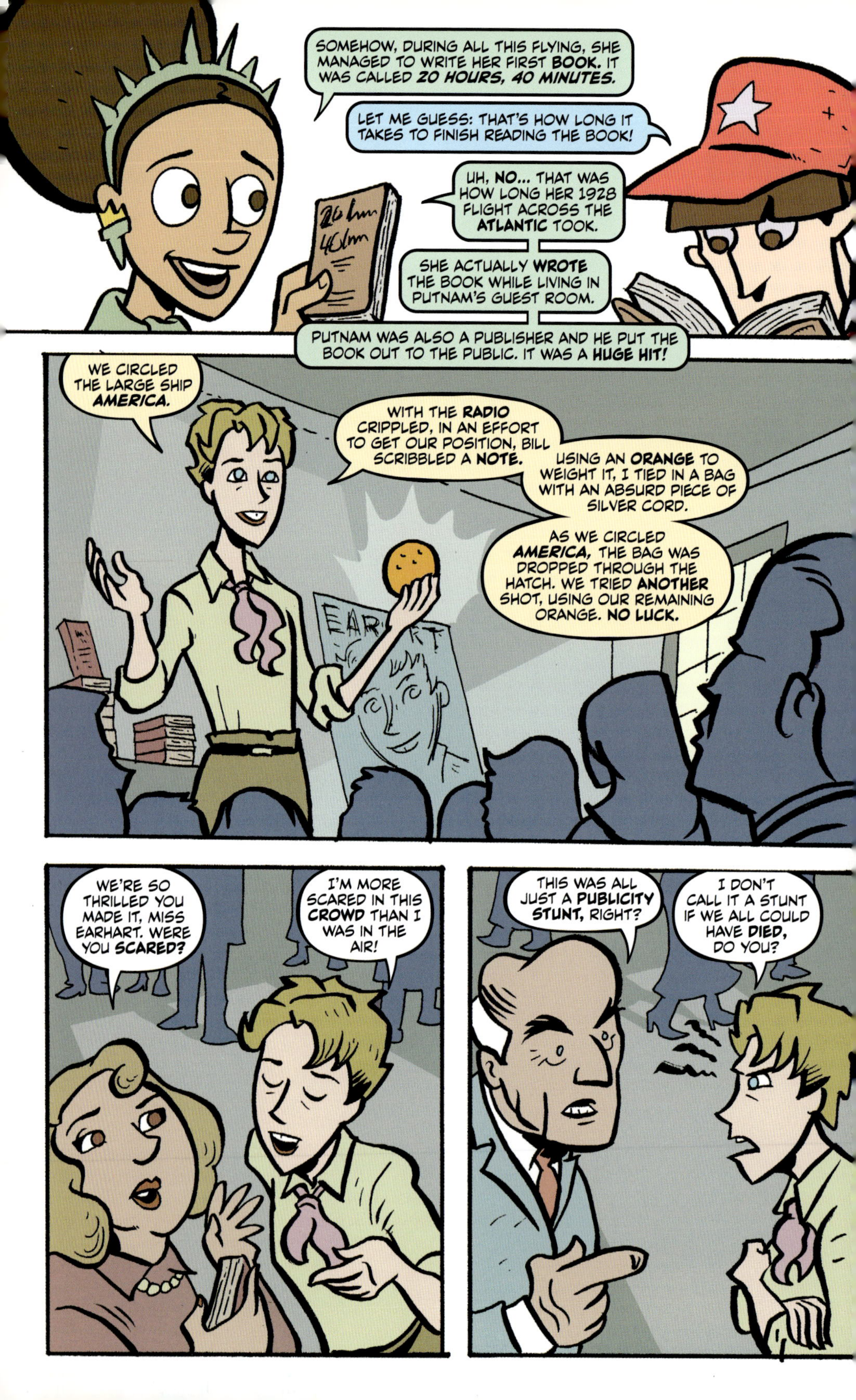
SOMEHOW, DURING ALL THIS FLYING, SHE MANAGED TO WRITE HER FIRST **BOOK.** IT WAS CALLED ***20 HOURS, 40 MINUTES.***
LET ME GUESS: THAT'S HOW LONG IT TAKES TO FINISH READING THE BOOK!
UH, **NO...** THAT WAS HOW LONG HER 1928 FLIGHT ACROSS THE **ATLANTIC** TOOK.
SHE ACTUALLY **WROTE** THE BOOK WHILE LIVING IN PUTNAM'S GUEST ROOM.
PUTNAM WAS ALSO A PUBLISHER AND HE PUT THE BOOK OUT TO THE PUBLIC. IT WAS A **HUGE HIT!**
WE CIRCLED THE LARGE SHIP ***AMERICA.***
WITH THE **RADIO** CRIPPLED, IN AN EFFORT TO GET OUR POSITION, BILL SCRIBBLED A **NOTE.**
USING AN **ORANGE** TO WEIGHT IT, I TIED IN A BAG WITH AN ABSURD PIECE OF SILVER CORD.
AS WE CIRCLED ***AMERICA,*** THE BAG WAS DROPPED THROUGH THE HATCH. WE TRIED **ANOTHER** SHOT, USING OUR REMAINING ORANGE. **NO LUCK.**
WE'RE SO THRILLED YOU MADE IT, MISS EARHART. WERE YOU **SCARED?**
I'M MORE SCARED IN THIS **CROWD** THAN I WAS IN THE AIR!
THIS WAS ALL JUST A **PUBLICITY STUNT,** RIGHT?
I DON'T CALL IT A STUNT IF WE ALL COULD HAVE **DIED,** DO YOU?

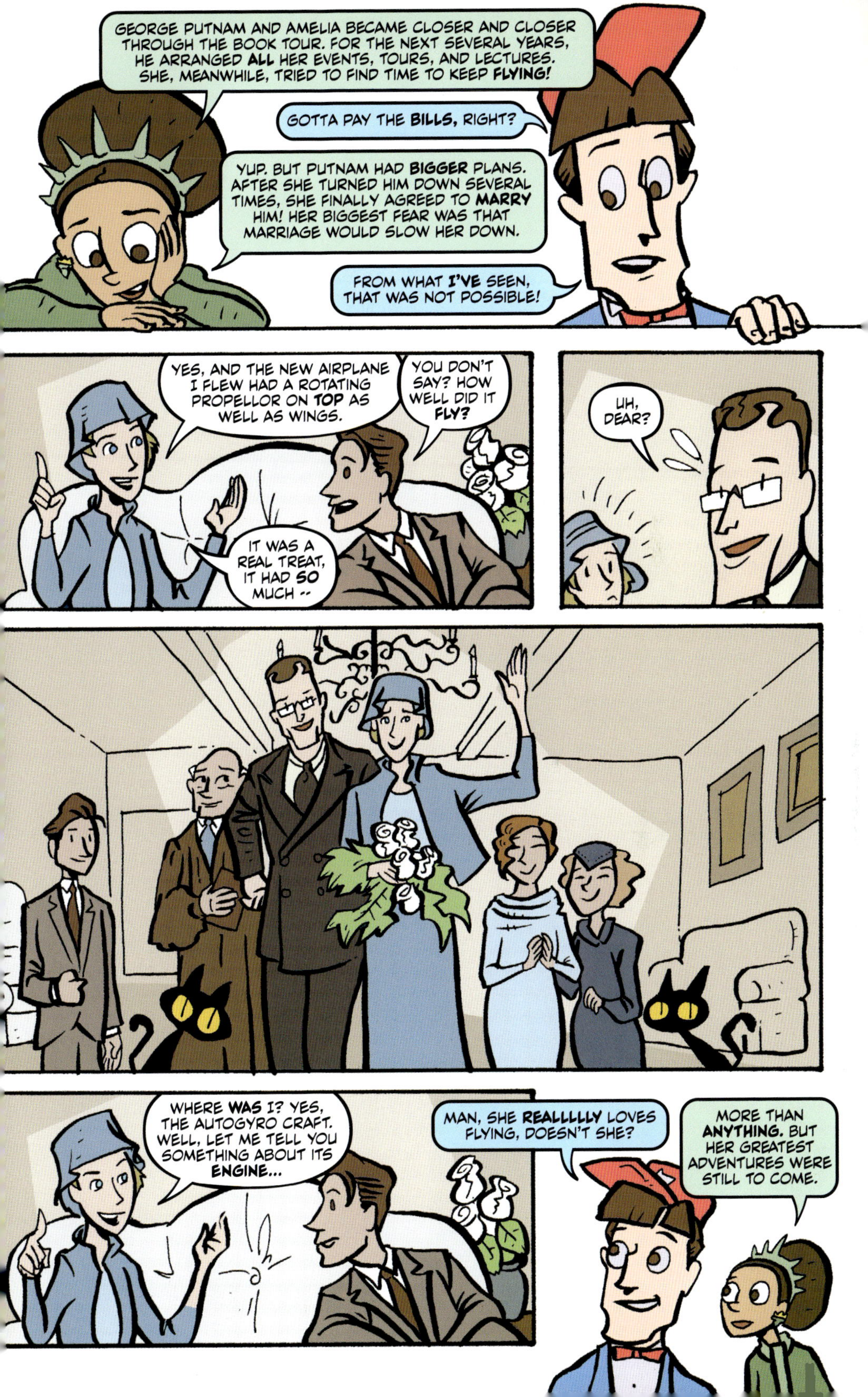
GEORGE PUTNAM AND AMELIA BECAME CLOSER AND CLOSER THROUGH THE BOOK TOUR. FOR THE NEXT SEVERAL YEARS, HE ARRANGED **ALL** HER EVENTS, TOURS, AND LECTURES. SHE, MEANWHILE, TRIED TO FIND TIME TO KEEP **FLYING!**
GOTTA PAY THE **BILLS,** RIGHT?
YUP. BUT PUTNAM HAD **BIGGER** PLANS. AFTER SHE TURNED HIM DOWN SEVERAL TIMES, SHE FINALLY AGREED TO **MARRY** HIM! HER BIGGEST FEAR WAS THAT MARRIAGE WOULD SLOW HER DOWN.
FROM WHAT **I'VE** SEEN, THAT WAS NOT POSSIBLE!
YES, AND THE NEW AIRPLANE I FLEW HAD A ROTATING PROPELLOR ON **TOP** AS WELL AS WINGS.
YOU DON'T SAY? HOW WELL DID IT **FLY?**
IT WAS A REAL TREAT, IT HAD **SO** MUCH --
UH, DEAR?
WHERE **WAS** I? YES, THE AUTOGYRO CRAFT. WELL, LET ME TELL YOU SOMETHING ABOUT ITS **ENGINE...**
MAN, SHE **REALLLLLY** LOVES FLYING, DOESN'T SHE?
MORE THAN **ANYTHING.** BUT HER GREATEST ADVENTURES WERE STILL TO COME.

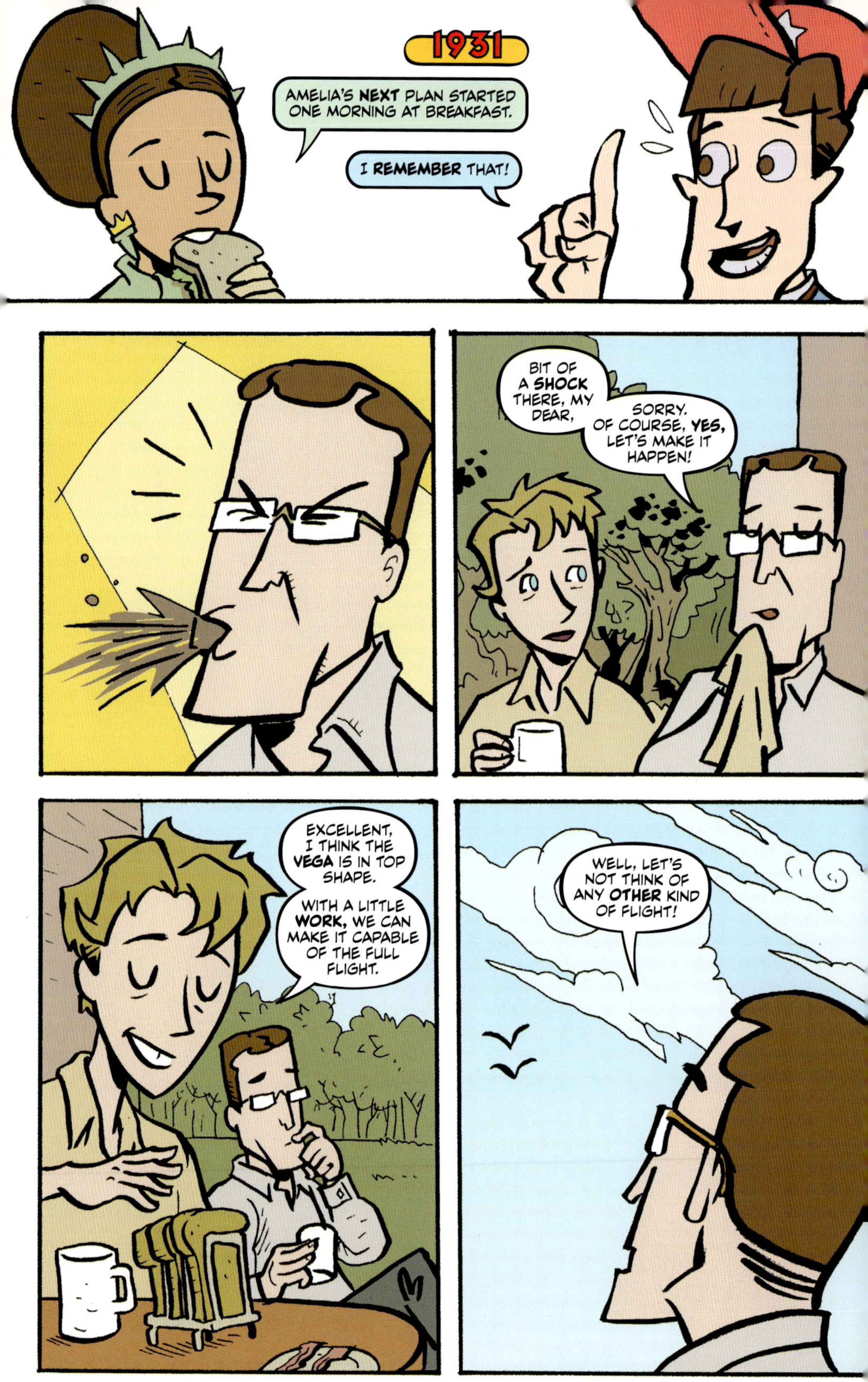

1931
AMELIA'S NEXT PLAN STARTED ONE MORNING AT BREAKFAST.
I REMEMBER THAT!
BIT OF A SHOCK THERE, MY DEAR,
SORRY. OF COURSE, YES, LET'S MAKE IT HAPPEN!
EXCELLENT, I THINK THE VEGA IS IN TOP SHAPE.
WITH A LITTLE WORK, WE CAN MAKE IT CAPABLE OF THE FULL FLIGHT.
WELL, LET'S NOT THINK OF ANY OTHER KIND OF FLIGHT!

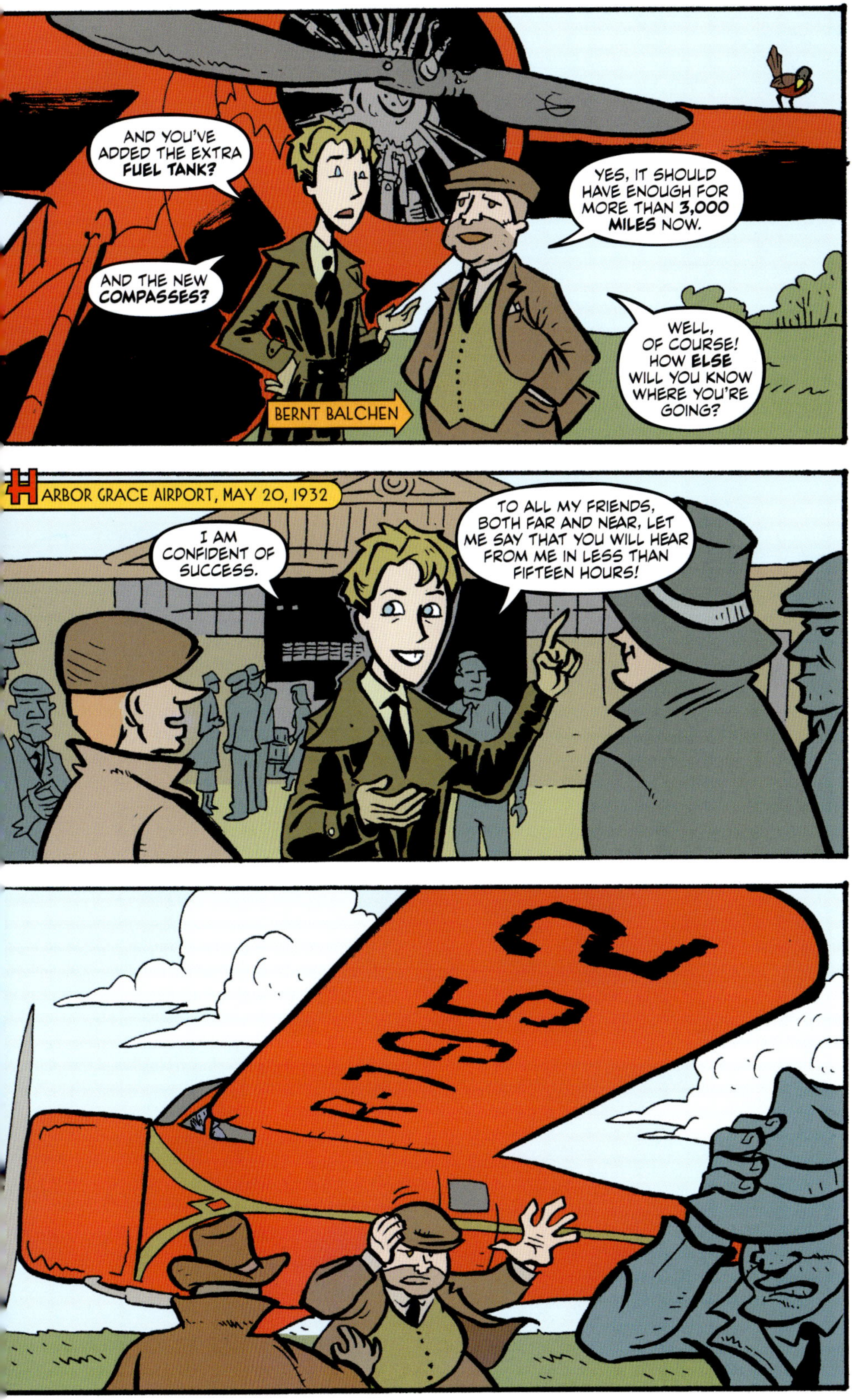
AND YOU'VE ADDED THE EXTRA FUEL TANK?
YES, IT SHOULD HAVE ENOUGH FOR MORE THAN 3,000 MILES NOW.
AND THE NEW COMPASSES?
WELL, OF COURSE! HOW ELSE WILL YOU KNOW WHERE YOU'RE GOING?
BERNT BALCHEN
HARBOR GRACE AIRPORT, MAY 20, 1932
I AM CONFIDENT OF SUCCESS.
TO ALL MY FRIENDS, BOTH FAR AND NEAR, LET ME SAY THAT YOU WILL HEAR FROM ME IN LESS THAN FIFTEEN HOURS!
R-7952

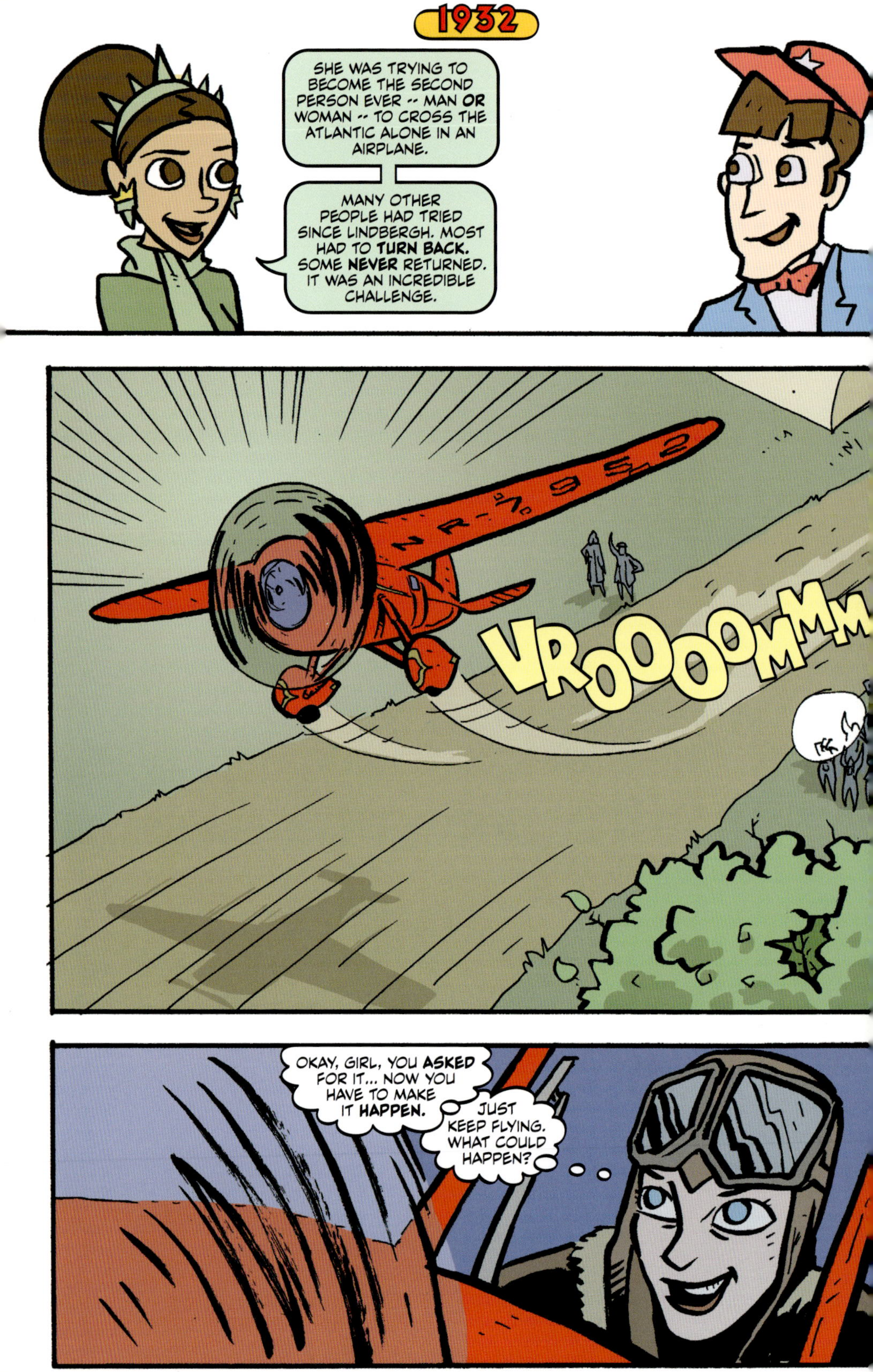
1932
SHE WAS TRYING TO BECOME THE SECOND PERSON EVER -- MAN OR WOMAN -- TO CROSS THE ATLANTIC ALONE IN AN AIRPLANE.
MANY OTHER PEOPLE HAD TRIED SINCE LINDBERGH. MOST HAD TO TURN BACK. SOME NEVER RETURNED. IT WAS AN INCREDIBLE CHALLENGE.
NR-7952
VROOOOMMM
OKAY, GIRL, YOU ASKED FOR IT... NOW YOU HAVE TO MAKE IT HAPPEN.
JUST KEEP FLYING. WHAT COULD HAPPEN?

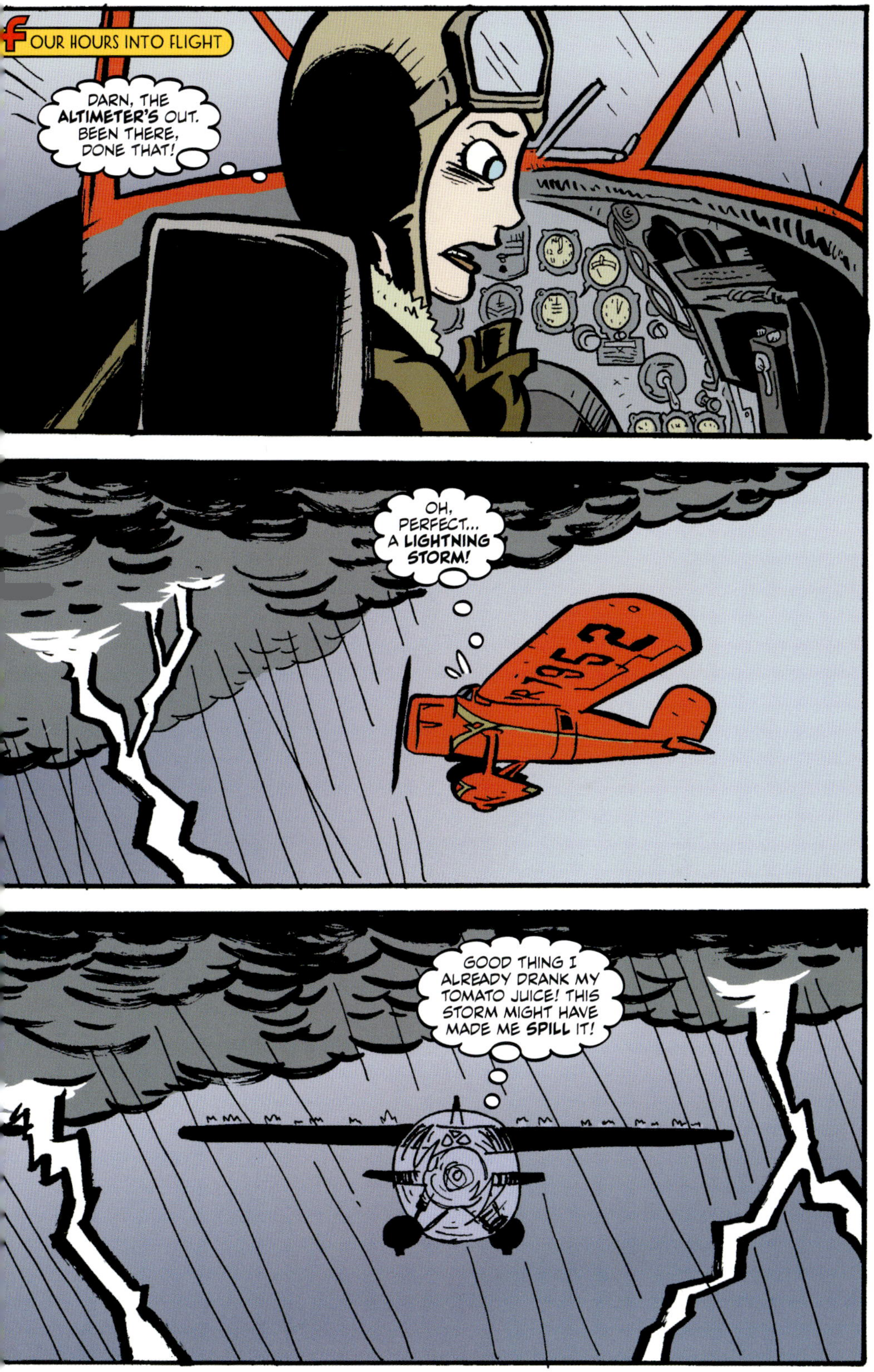
FOUR HOURS INTO FLIGHT
DARN, THE ALTIMETER'S OUT. BEEN THERE, DONE THAT!
OH, PERFECT... A LIGHTNING STORM!
R1952
GOOD THING I ALREADY DRANK MY TOMATO JUICE! THIS STORM MIGHT HAVE MADE ME SPILL IT!

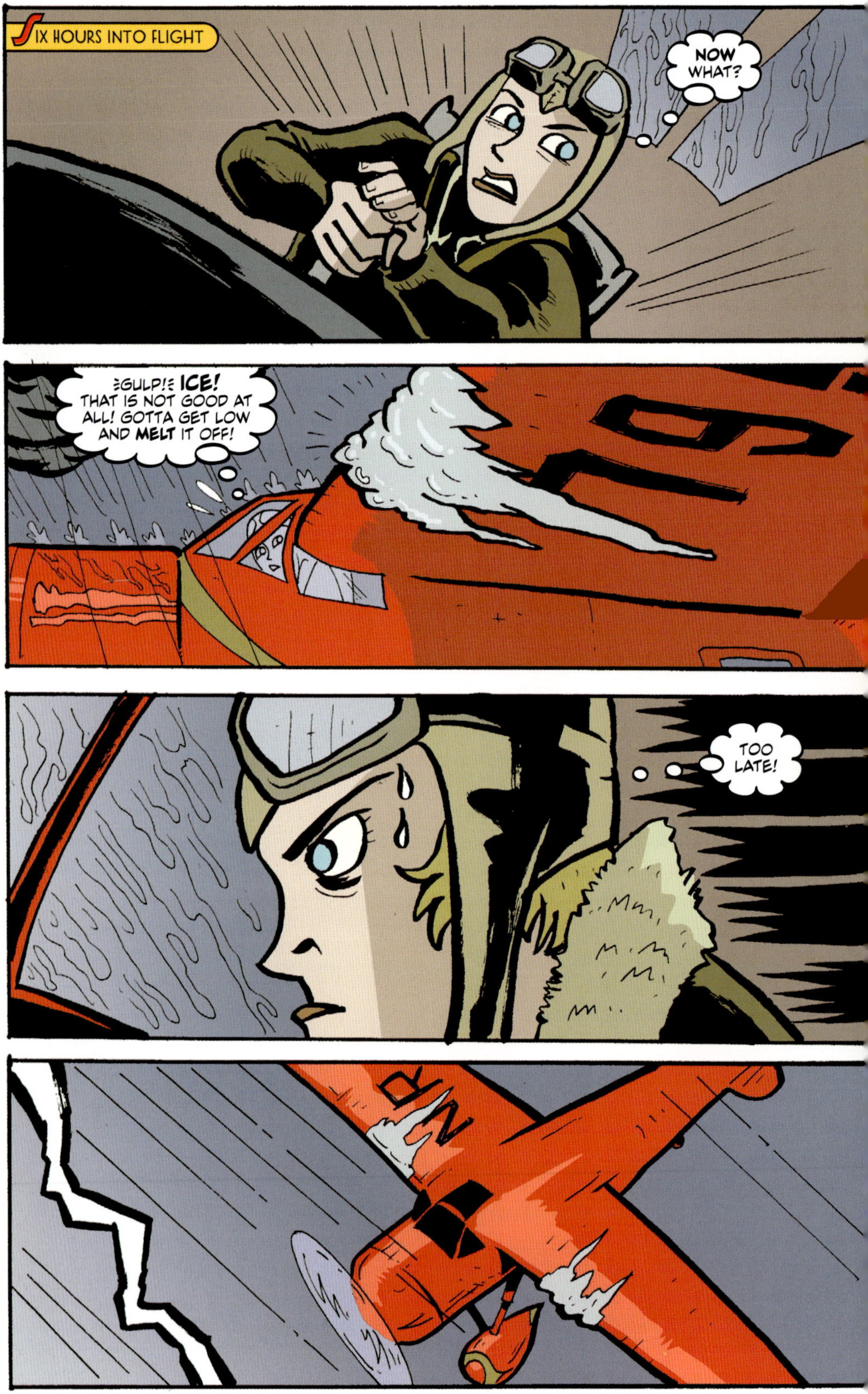
SIX HOURS INTO FLIGHT
NOW WHAT?
GULP! ICE! THAT IS NOT GOOD AT ALL! GOTTA GET LOW AND MELT IT OFF!
TOO LATE!

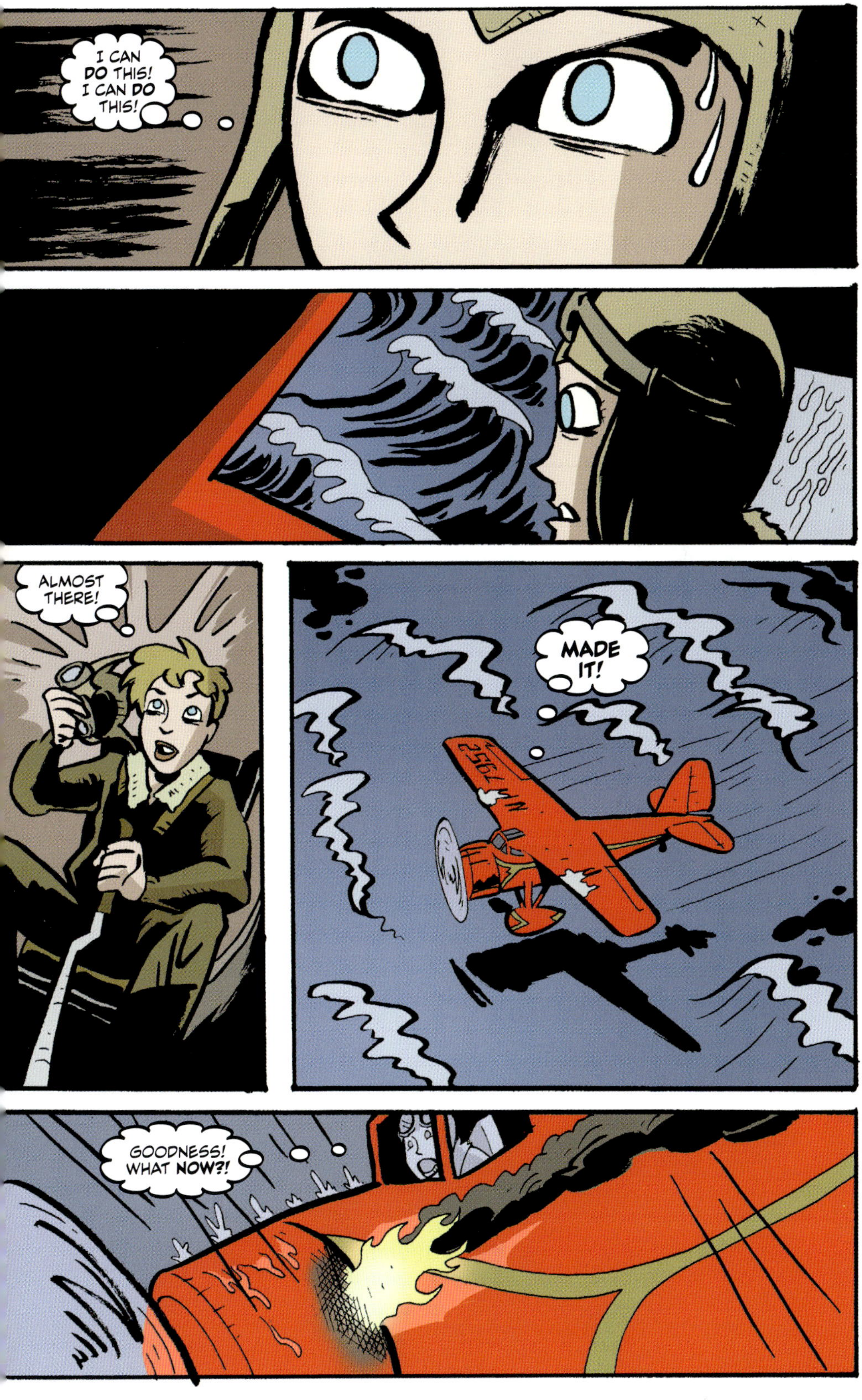
I CAN DO THIS! I CAN DO THIS!
ALMOST THERE!
MADE IT!
GOODNESS! WHAT NOW?!

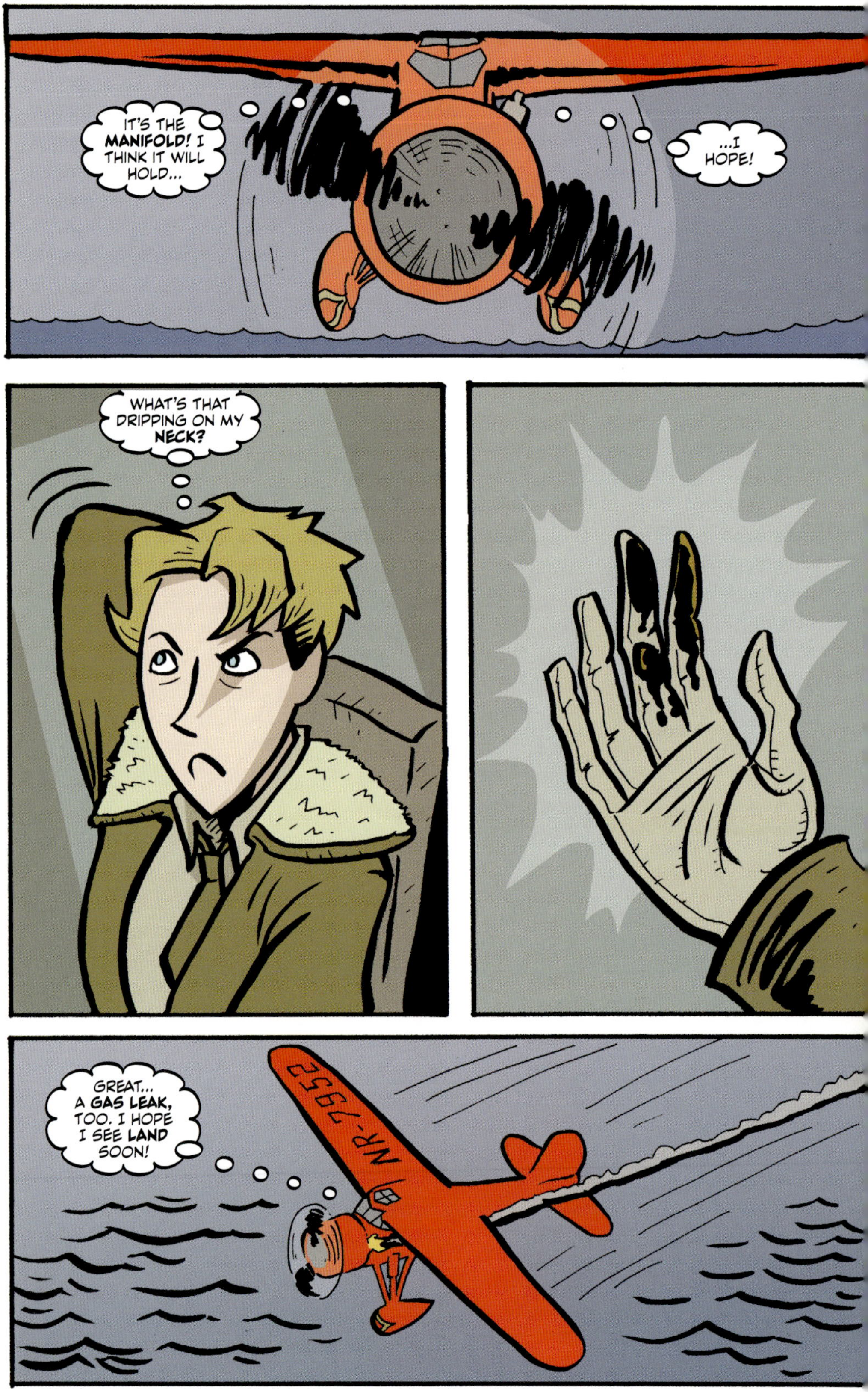
IT'S THE **MANIFOLD!** I THINK IT WILL HOLD...
...I HOPE!
WHAT'S THAT DRIPPING ON MY **NECK?**
GREAT... A **GAS LEAK,** TOO. I HOPE I SEE **LAND** SOON!
NR-7952

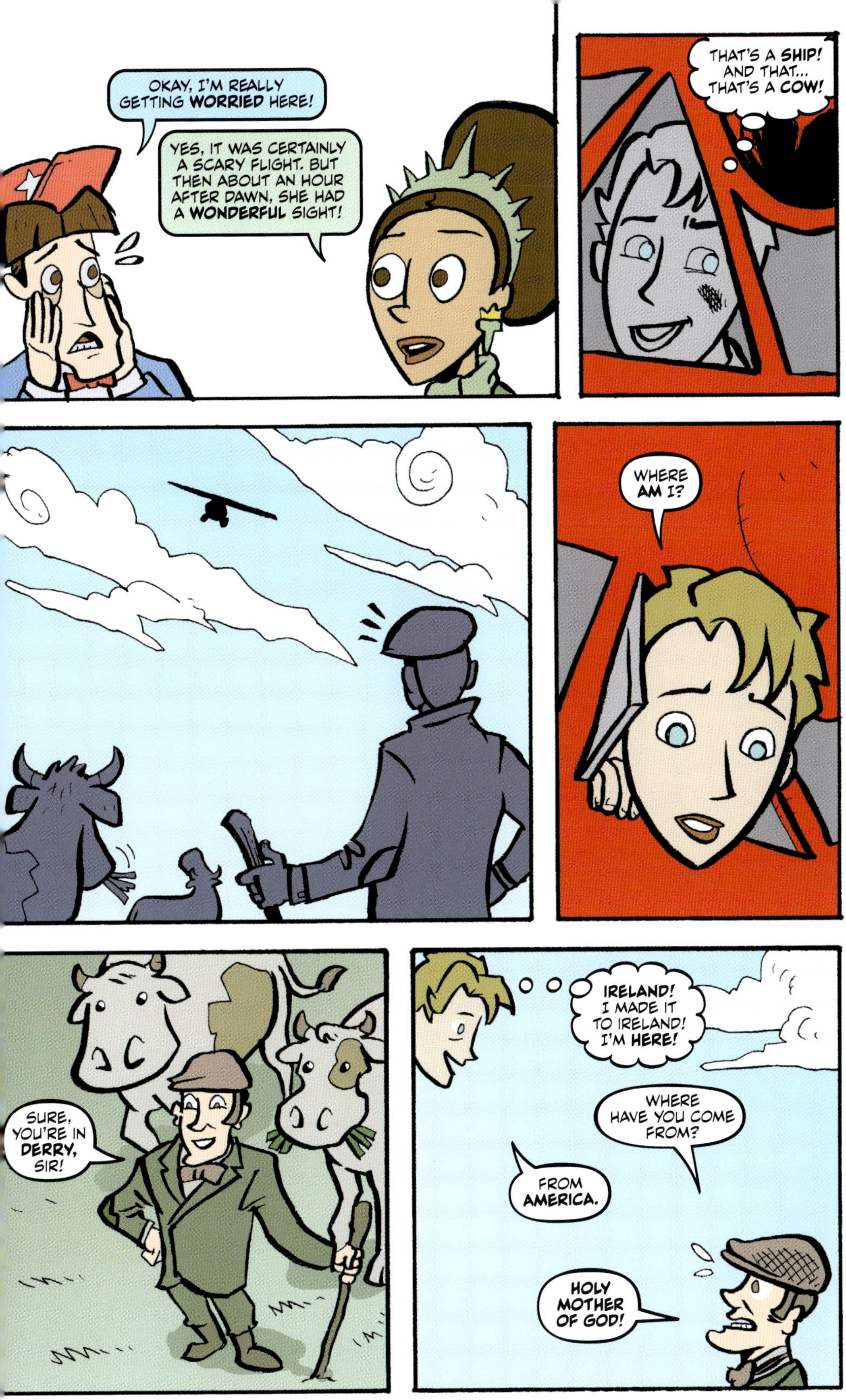
OKAY, I'M REALLY GETTING WORRIED HERE!
YES, IT WAS CERTAINLY A SCARY FLIGHT. BUT THEN ABOUT AN HOUR AFTER DAWN, SHE HAD A WONDERFUL SIGHT!
THAT'S A SHIP! AND THAT... THAT'S A COW!
WHERE AM I?
SURE, YOU'RE IN DERRY, SIR!
IRELAND! I MADE IT TO IRELAND! I'M HERE!
WHERE HAVE YOU COME FROM?
FROM AMERICA.
HOLY MOTHER OF GOD!

YES, SHE HAD **DONE** IT. AMELIA HAD BECOME THE FIRST WOMAN TO FLY ACROSS THE **ATLANTIC OCEAN.** SHE WAS PROVING THAT THERE WAS **NOTHING** THAT WOMEN COULD NOT DO!

WOO-HOO! GOOD FOR HER! I BET SHE WAS PRETTY **POPULAR...** AGAIN.

SAM, YOU HAVE **NO IDEA!** IT WAS EVEN **BIGGER** AND **WILDER** THAN IT HAD BEEN IN 1928.

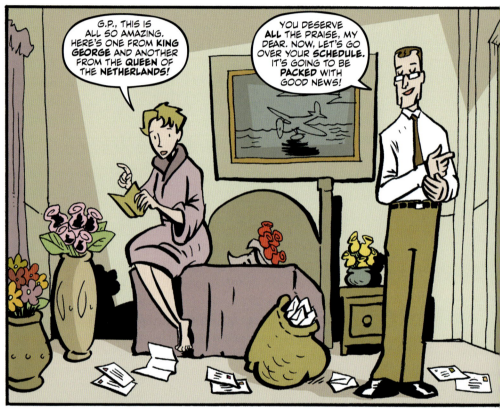

G.P., THIS IS ALL SO AMAZING. HERE'S ONE FROM **KING GEORGE** AND ANOTHER FROM THE **QUEEN** OF THE **NETHERLANDS!**

YOU DESERVE **ALL** THE PRAISE, MY DEAR. NOW, LET'S GO OVER YOUR **SCHEDULE.** IT'S GOING TO BE **PACKED** WITH GOOD NEWS!

REMEMBER, THOUGH, YOU **PROMISED** I WOULD NOT HAVE TO GIVE UP FLYING TO **BE** WITH YOU!

I'LL NEVER **FORGET** THAT!

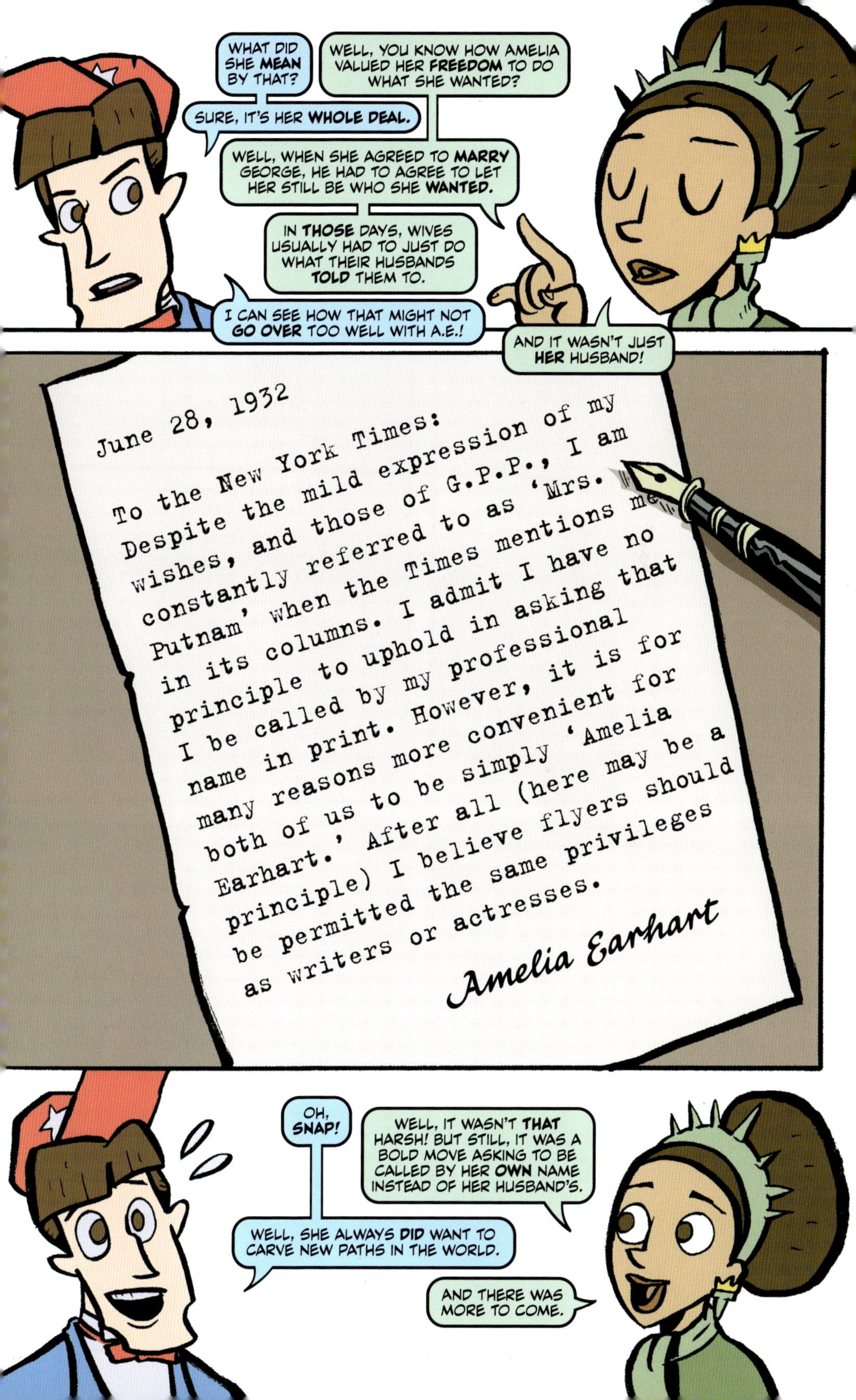
WHAT DID SHE MEAN BY THAT?
WELL, YOU KNOW HOW AMELIA VALUED HER FREEDOM TO DO WHAT SHE WANTED?
SURE, IT'S HER WHOLE DEAL.
WELL, WHEN SHE AGREED TO MARRY GEORGE, HE HAD TO AGREE TO LET HER STILL BE WHO SHE WANTED.
IN THOSE DAYS, WIVES USUALLY HAD TO JUST DO WHAT THEIR HUSBANDS TOLD THEM TO.
I CAN SEE HOW THAT MIGHT NOT GO OVER TOO WELL WITH A.E.!
AND IT WASN'T JUST HER HUSBAND!
June 28, 1932
To the New York Times:
Despite the mild expression of my wishes, and those of G.P.P., I am constantly referred to as 'Mrs. Putnam' when the Times mentions me in its columns. I admit I have no principle to uphold in asking that I be called by my professional name in print. However, it is for many reasons more convenient for both of us to be simply 'Amelia Earhart.' After all (here may be a principle) I believe flyers should be permitted the same privileges as writers or actresses.
Amelia Earhart
OH, SNAP!
WELL, IT WASN'T THAT HARSH! BUT STILL, IT WAS A BOLD MOVE ASKING TO BE CALLED BY HER OWN NAME INSTEAD OF HER HUSBAND'S.
WELL, SHE ALWAYS DID WANT TO CARVE NEW PATHS IN THE WORLD.
AND THERE WAS MORE TO COME.

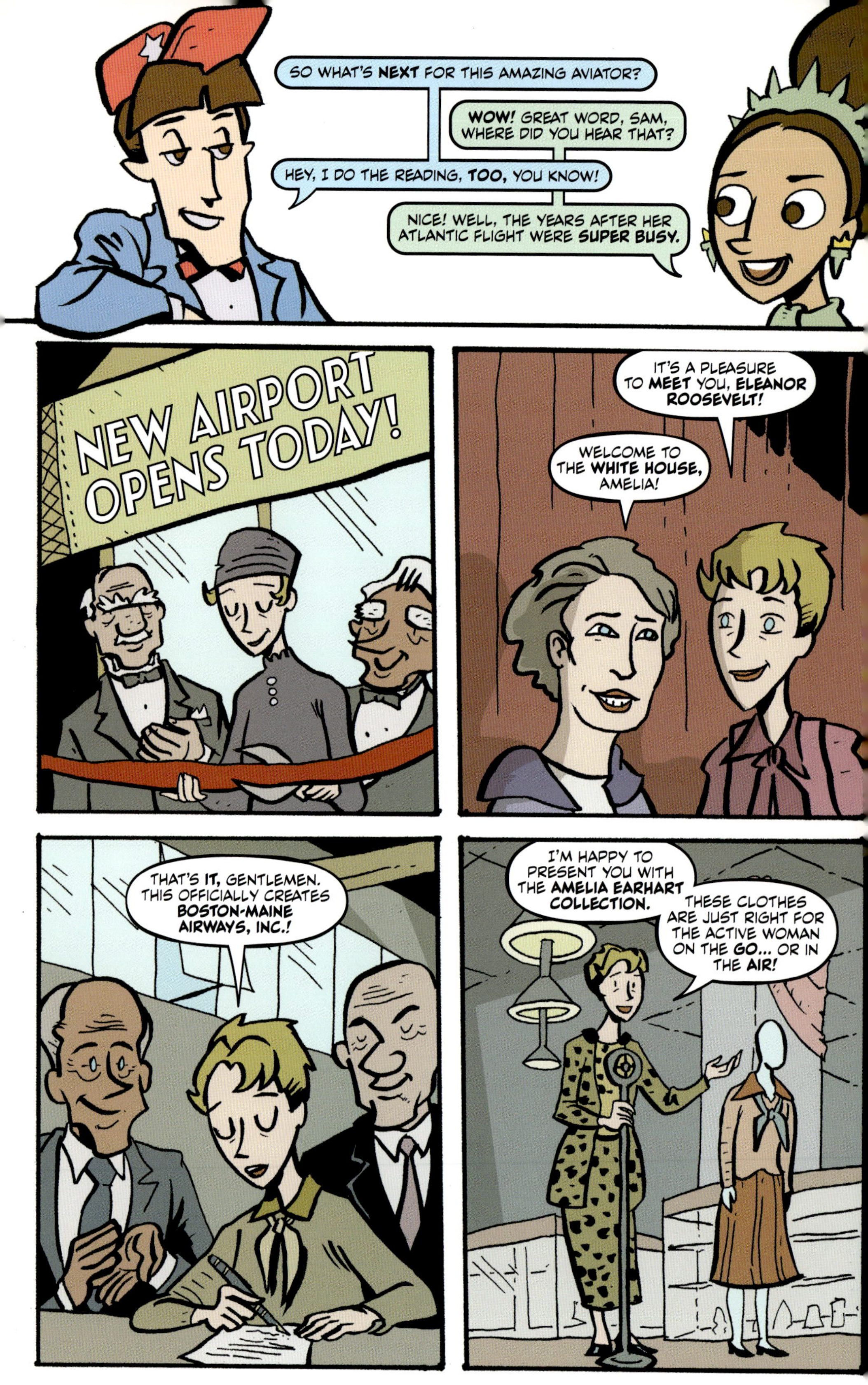
SO WHAT'S NEXT FOR THIS AMAZING AVIATOR?
WOW! GREAT WORD, SAM, WHERE DID YOU HEAR THAT?
HEY, I DO THE READING, TOO, YOU KNOW!
NICE! WELL, THE YEARS AFTER HER ATLANTIC FLIGHT WERE SUPER BUSY.
NEW AIRPORT OPENS TODAY!
IT'S A PLEASURE TO MEET YOU, ELEANOR ROOSEVELT!
WELCOME TO THE WHITE HOUSE, AMELIA!
THAT'S IT, GENTLEMEN. THIS OFFICIALLY CREATES BOSTON-MAINE AIRWAYS, INC.!
I'M HAPPY TO PRESENT YOU WITH THE AMELIA EARHART COLLECTION.
THESE CLOTHES ARE JUST RIGHT FOR THE ACTIVE WOMAN ON THE GO... OR IN THE AIR!

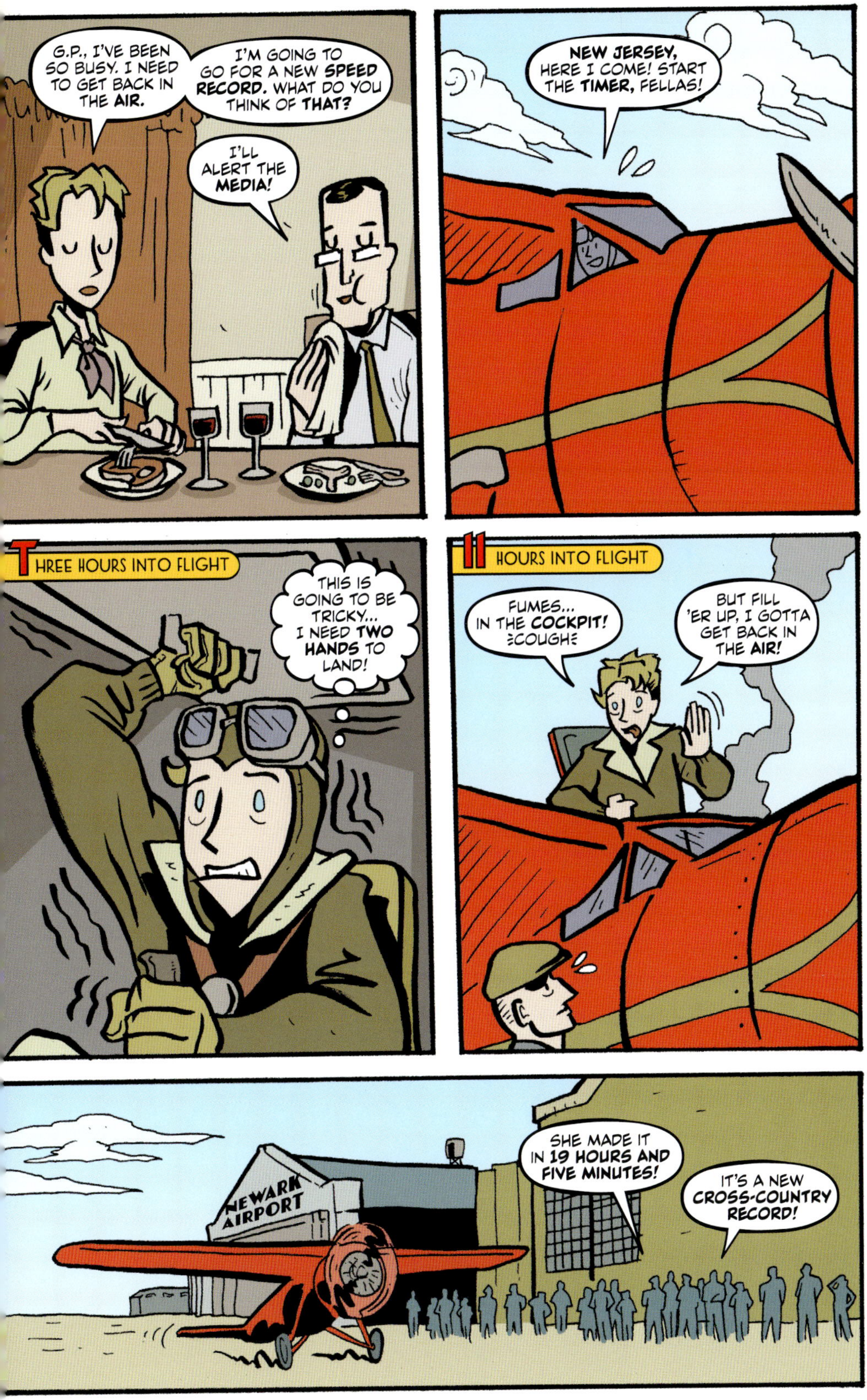
G.P., I'VE BEEN SO BUSY. I NEED TO GET BACK IN THE AIR.
I'M GOING TO GO FOR A NEW SPEED RECORD. WHAT DO YOU THINK OF THAT?
I'LL ALERT THE MEDIA!
NEW JERSEY, HERE I COME! START THE TIMER, FELLAS!
THREE HOURS INTO FLIGHT
THIS IS GOING TO BE TRICKY... I NEED TWO HANDS TO LAND!
11 HOURS INTO FLIGHT
FUMES... IN THE COCKPIT! COUGH
BUT FILL 'ER UP, I GOTTA GET BACK IN THE AIR!
NEWARK AIRPORT
SHE MADE IT IN 19 HOURS AND FIVE MINUTES!
IT'S A NEW CROSS-COUNTRY RECORD!

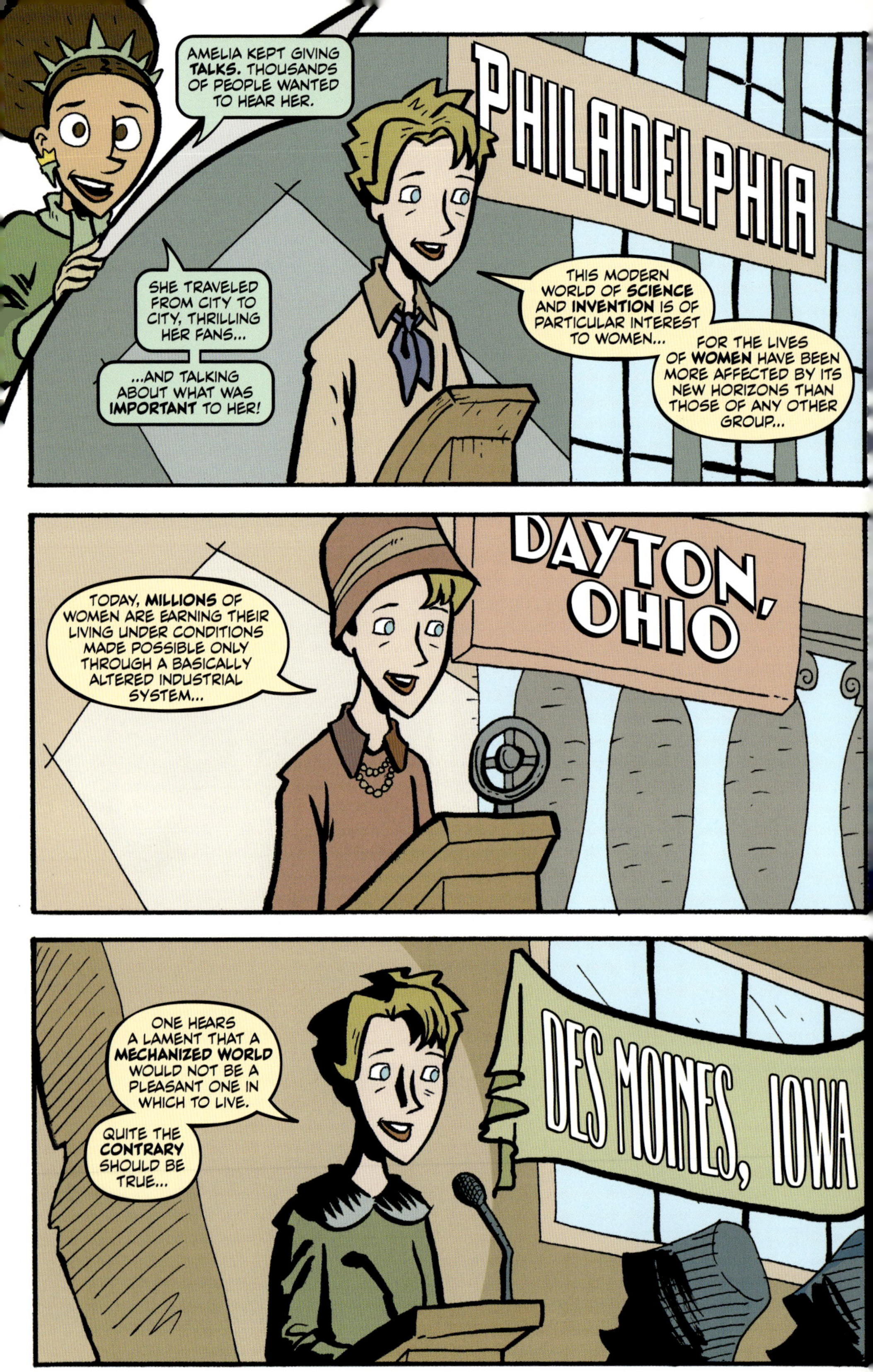
AMELIA KEPT GIVING **TALKS.** THOUSANDS OF PEOPLE WANTED TO HEAR HER.
PHILADELPHIA
SHE TRAVELED FROM CITY TO CITY, THRILLING HER FANS...
...AND TALKING ABOUT WHAT WAS **IMPORTANT** TO HER!
THIS MODERN WORLD OF **SCIENCE** AND **INVENTION** IS OF PARTICULAR INTEREST TO WOMEN...
FOR THE LIVES OF **WOMEN** HAVE BEEN MORE AFFECTED BY ITS NEW HORIZONS THAN THOSE OF ANY OTHER GROUP...
DAYTON, OHIO
TODAY, **MILLIONS** OF WOMEN ARE EARNING THEIR LIVING UNDER CONDITIONS MADE POSSIBLE ONLY THROUGH A BASICALLY ALTERED INDUSTRIAL SYSTEM...
DES MOINES, IOWA
ONE HEARS A LAMENT THAT A **MECHANIZED WORLD** WOULD NOT BE A PLEASANT ONE IN WHICH TO LIVE.
QUITE THE **CONTRARY** SHOULD BE TRUE...

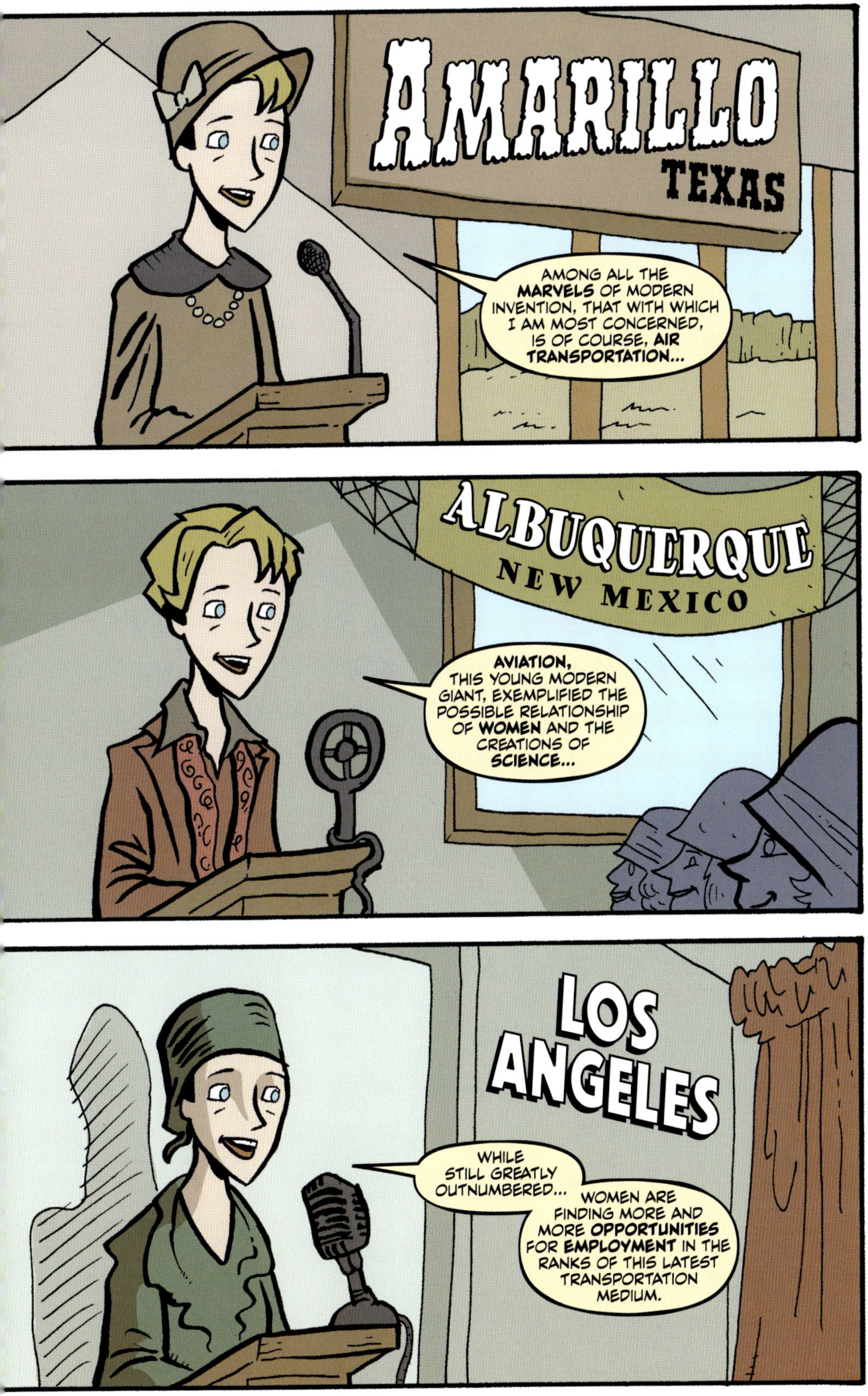
AMARILLO
TEXAS
AMONG ALL THE **MARVELS** OF MODERN INVENTION, THAT WITH WHICH I AM MOST CONCERNED, IS OF COURSE, **AIR TRANSPORTATION...**
ALBUQUERQUE
NEW MEXICO
AVIATION, THIS YOUNG MODERN GIANT, EXEMPLIFIED THE POSSIBLE RELATIONSHIP OF **WOMEN** AND THE CREATIONS OF **SCIENCE...**
LOS ANGELES
WHILE STILL GREATLY OUTNUMBERED...
WOMEN ARE FINDING MORE AND MORE **OPPORTUNITIES** FOR **EMPLOYMENT** IN THE RANKS OF THIS LATEST TRANSPORTATION MEDIUM.

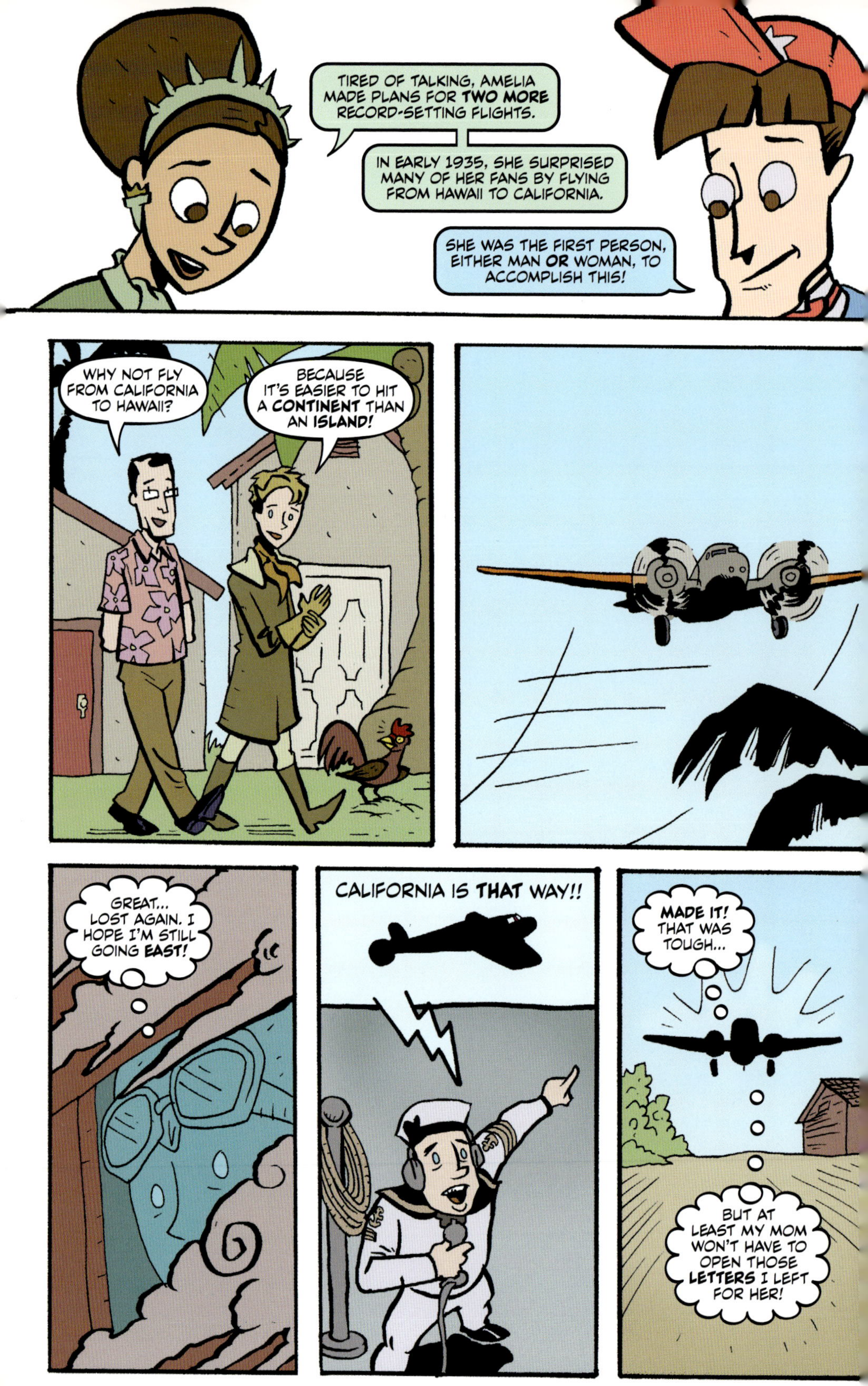
TIRED OF TALKING, AMELIA MADE PLANS FOR **TWO MORE** RECORD-SETTING FLIGHTS.
IN EARLY 1935, SHE SURPRISED MANY OF HER FANS BY FLYING FROM HAWAII TO CALIFORNIA.
SHE WAS THE FIRST PERSON, EITHER MAN **OR** WOMAN, TO ACCOMPLISH THIS!
WHY NOT FLY FROM CALIFORNIA TO HAWAII?
BECAUSE IT'S EASIER TO HIT A **CONTINENT** THAN AN **ISLAND!**
GREAT... LOST AGAIN. I HOPE I'M STILL GOING **EAST!**
CALIFORNIA IS **THAT** WAY!!
MADE IT! THAT WAS TOUGH...
BUT AT LEAST MY MOM WON'T HAVE TO OPEN THOSE **LETTERS** I LEFT FOR HER!

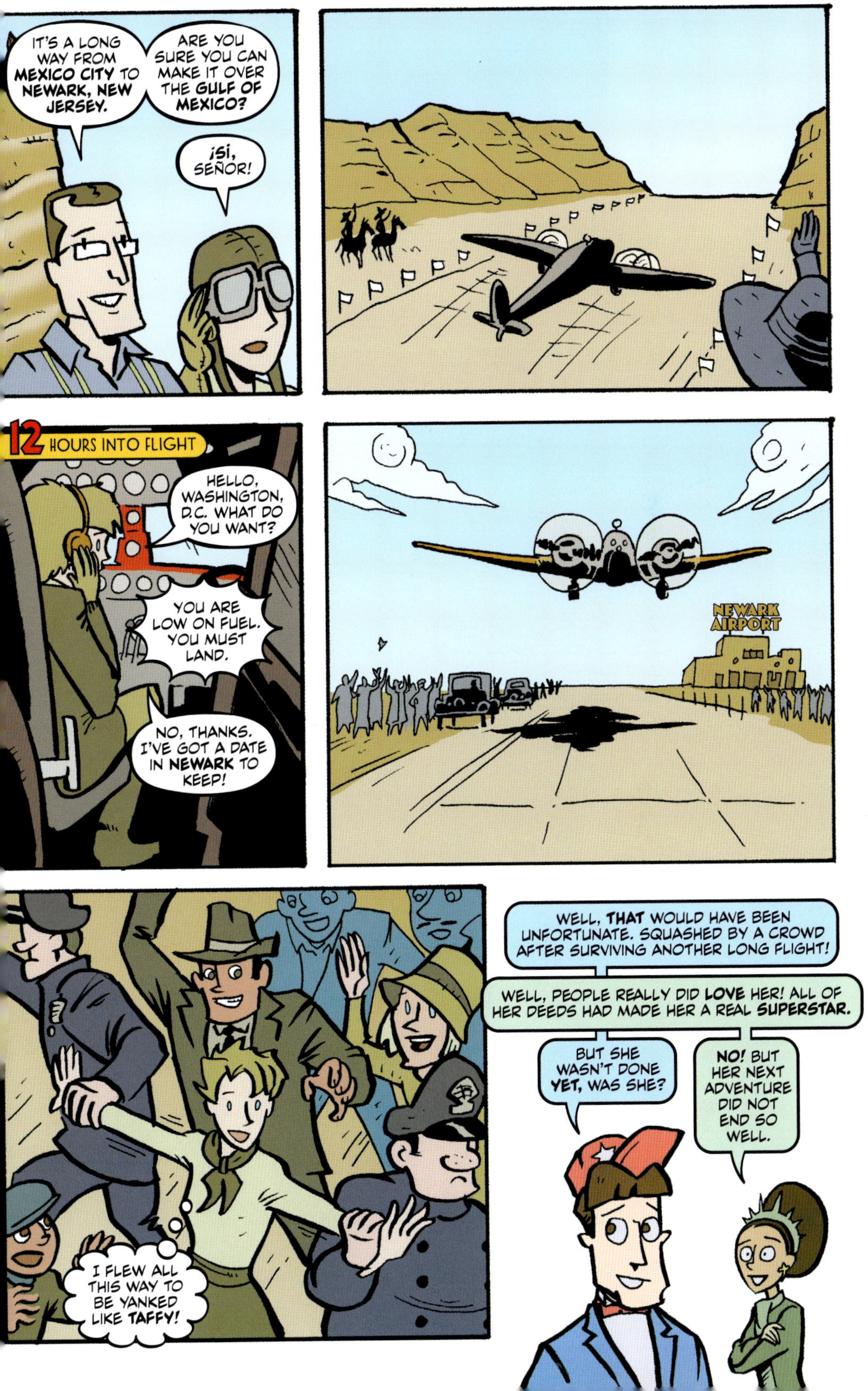
IT'S A LONG WAY FROM MEXICO CITY TO NEWARK, NEW JERSEY.
ARE YOU SURE YOU CAN MAKE IT OVER THE GULF OF MEXICO?
¡SÍ, SEÑOR!
12 HOURS INTO FLIGHT
HELLO, WASHINGTON, D.C. WHAT DO YOU WANT?
YOU ARE LOW ON FUEL. YOU MUST LAND.
NO, THANKS. I'VE GOT A DATE IN NEWARK TO KEEP!
NEWARK AIRPORT
I FLEW ALL THIS WAY TO BE YANKED LIKE TAFFY!
WELL, THAT WOULD HAVE BEEN UNFORTUNATE. SQUASHED BY A CROWD AFTER SURVIVING ANOTHER LONG FLIGHT!
WELL, PEOPLE REALLY DID LOVE HER! ALL OF HER DEEDS HAD MADE HER A REAL SUPERSTAR.
BUT SHE WASN'T DONE YET, WAS SHE?
NO! BUT HER NEXT ADVENTURE DID NOT END SO WELL.

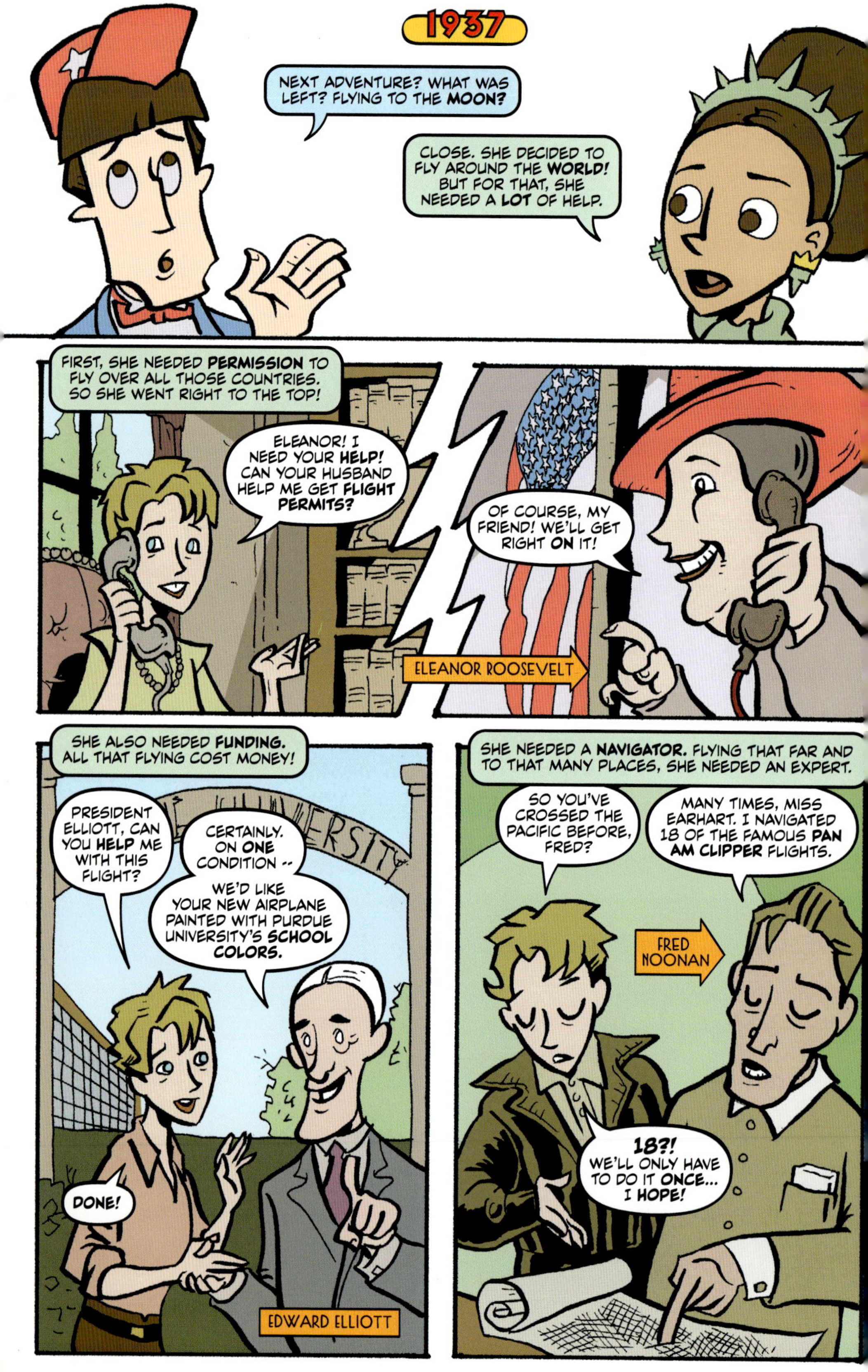
1937
NEXT ADVENTURE? WHAT WAS LEFT? FLYING TO THE MOON?
CLOSE. SHE DECIDED TO FLY AROUND THE WORLD! BUT FOR THAT, SHE NEEDED A LOT OF HELP.
FIRST, SHE NEEDED PERMISSION TO FLY OVER ALL THOSE COUNTRIES. SO SHE WENT RIGHT TO THE TOP!
ELEANOR! I NEED YOUR HELP! CAN YOUR HUSBAND HELP ME GET FLIGHT PERMITS?
OF COURSE, MY FRIEND! WE'LL GET RIGHT ON IT!
ELEANOR ROOSEVELT
SHE ALSO NEEDED FUNDING. ALL THAT FLYING COST MONEY!
PRESIDENT ELLIOTT, CAN YOU HELP ME WITH THIS FLIGHT?
CERTAINLY. ON ONE CONDITION --
WE'D LIKE YOUR NEW AIRPLANE PAINTED WITH PURDUE UNIVERSITY'S SCHOOL COLORS.
DONE!
EDWARD ELLIOTT
SHE NEEDED A NAVIGATOR. FLYING THAT FAR AND TO THAT MANY PLACES, SHE NEEDED AN EXPERT.
SO YOU'VE CROSSED THE PACIFIC BEFORE, FRED?
MANY TIMES, MISS EARHART. I NAVIGATED 18 OF THE FAMOUS PAN AM CLIPPER FLIGHTS.
FRED NOONAN
18?! WE'LL ONLY HAVE TO DO IT ONCE... I HOPE!

THE PLAN WAS TO FLY FROM **EAST** TO **WEST**. THEY WOULD TAKE OFF FROM **OAKLAND** AND FLY FIRST TO **HAWAII**. THEN THEY WOULD MAKE THE LONG, DANGEROUS TRIP ACROSS THE **FAR PACIFIC**.

WAIT... **DANGEROUS?**

OTHERS HAD **TRIED** BUT NONE OF THEM HAD **MADE** IT.

OH.

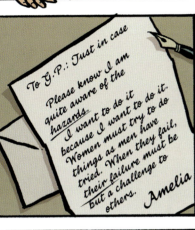

To G.P.: Just in case

Please know I am quite aware of the hazards.

I want to do it because I want to do it. Women must try to do things as men have tried. When they fail, their failure must be but a challenge to others.

Amelia

OKAY, FRED, HERE WE GO!

WELCOME TO **HAWAI'I** LAND OF PINEAPPLES

GOTTA SHUT OFF THE GAS QUICK!

FUEL

I HIT A **WET SPOT**. THE SHIP WENT OFF COURSE AND I COULDN'T STOP IT.

AT LEAST EVERYONE IS **OKAY**.

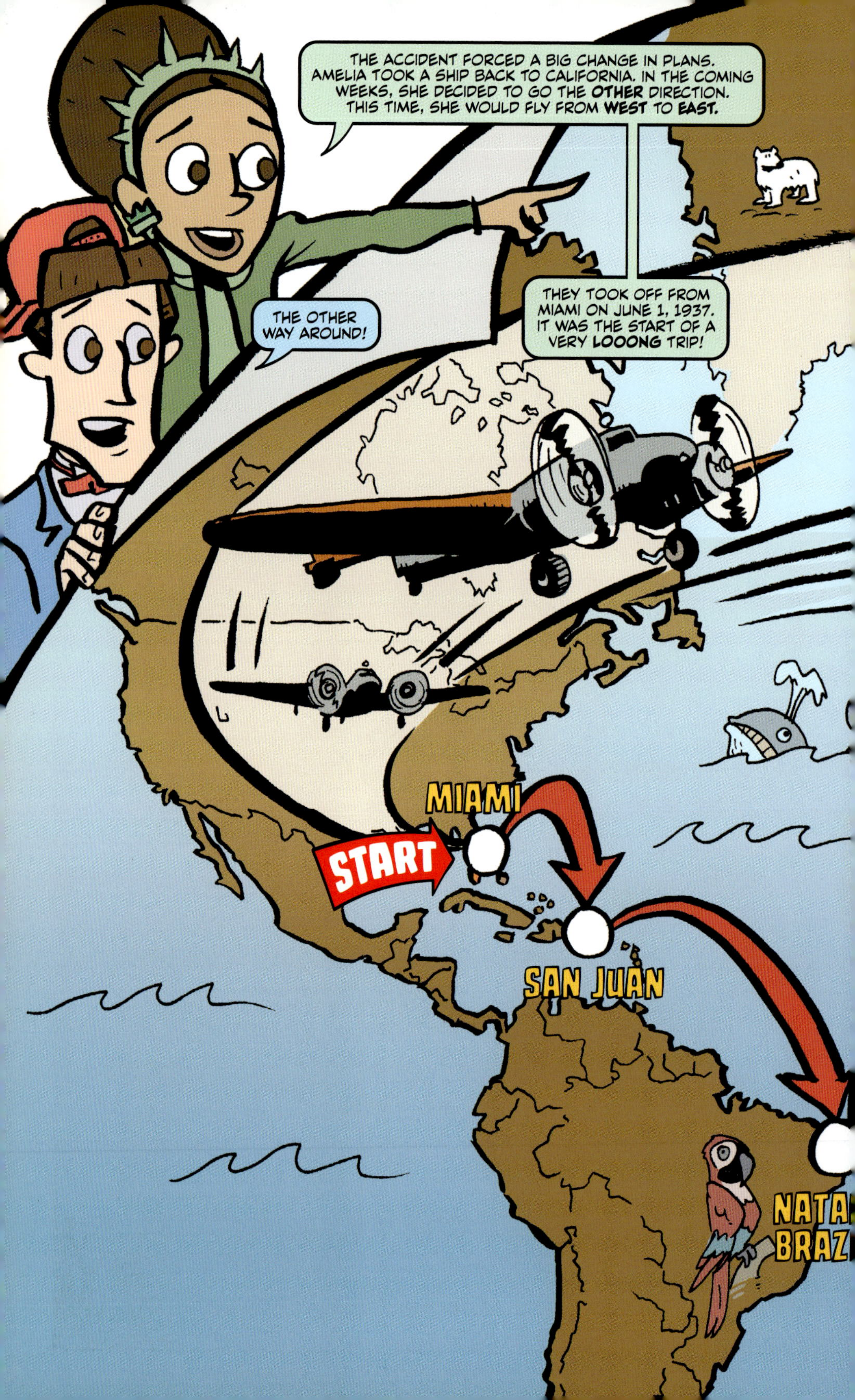
THE ACCIDENT FORCED A BIG CHANGE IN PLANS. AMELIA TOOK A SHIP BACK TO CALIFORNIA. IN THE COMING WEEKS, SHE DECIDED TO GO THE **OTHER** DIRECTION. THIS TIME, SHE WOULD FLY FROM **WEST** TO **EAST.**
THE OTHER WAY AROUND!
THEY TOOK OFF FROM MIAMI ON JUNE 1, 1937. IT WAS THE START OF A VERY **LOOONG** TRIP!
MIAMI
START
SAN JUAN

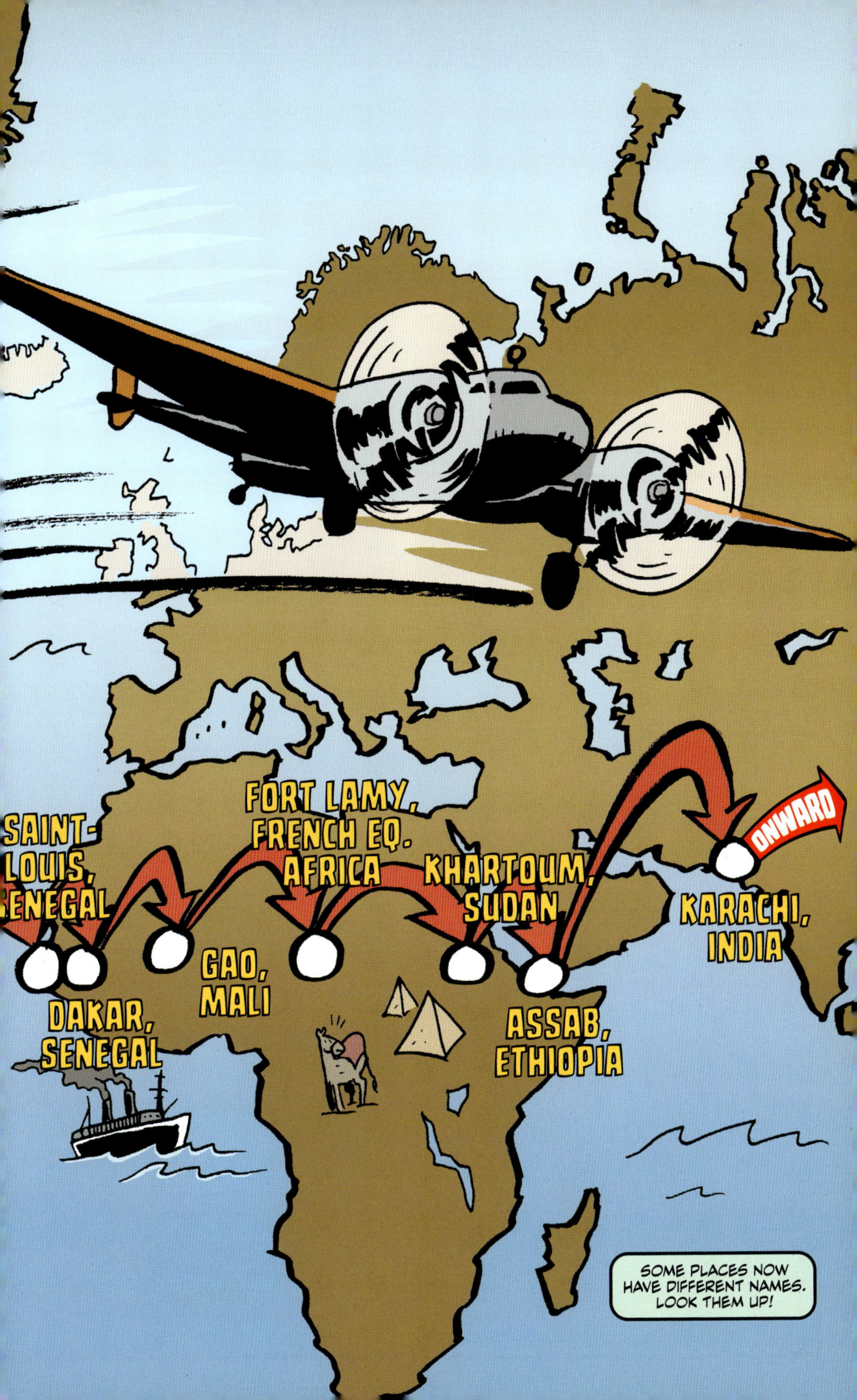
SAINT-LOUIS, SENEGAL
DAKAR, SENEGAL
GAO, MALI
FORT LAMY, FRENCH EQ. AFRICA
KHARTOUM, SUDAN
ASSAB, ETHIOPIA
KARACHI, INDIA
ONWARD
SOME PLACES NOW HAVE DIFFERENT NAMES. LOOK THEM UP!

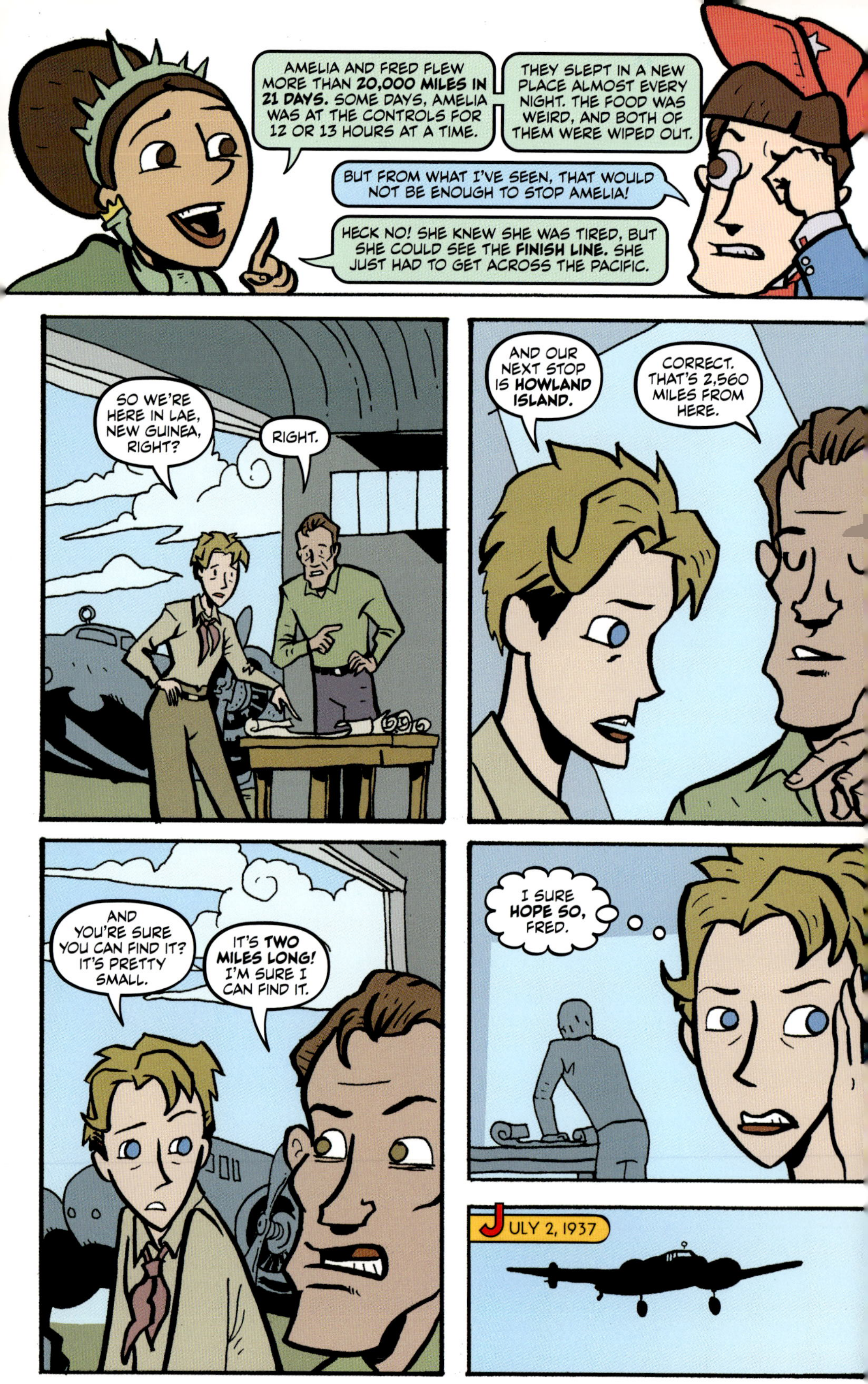
AMELIA AND FRED FLEW MORE THAN **20,000 MILES IN 21 DAYS.** SOME DAYS, AMELIA WAS AT THE CONTROLS FOR 12 OR 13 HOURS AT A TIME.
THEY SLEPT IN A NEW PLACE ALMOST EVERY NIGHT. THE FOOD WAS WEIRD, AND BOTH OF THEM WERE WIPED OUT.
BUT FROM WHAT I'VE SEEN, THAT WOULD NOT BE ENOUGH TO STOP AMELIA!
HECK NO! SHE KNEW SHE WAS TIRED, BUT SHE COULD SEE THE **FINISH LINE.** SHE JUST HAD TO GET ACROSS THE PACIFIC.
SO WE'RE HERE IN LAE, NEW GUINEA, RIGHT?
RIGHT.
AND OUR NEXT STOP IS **HOWLAND ISLAND.**
CORRECT. THAT'S 2,560 MILES FROM HERE.
AND YOU'RE SURE YOU CAN FIND IT? IT'S PRETTY SMALL.
IT'S **TWO MILES LONG!** I'M SURE I CAN FIND IT.
I SURE **HOPE SO,** FRED.
JULY 2, 1937

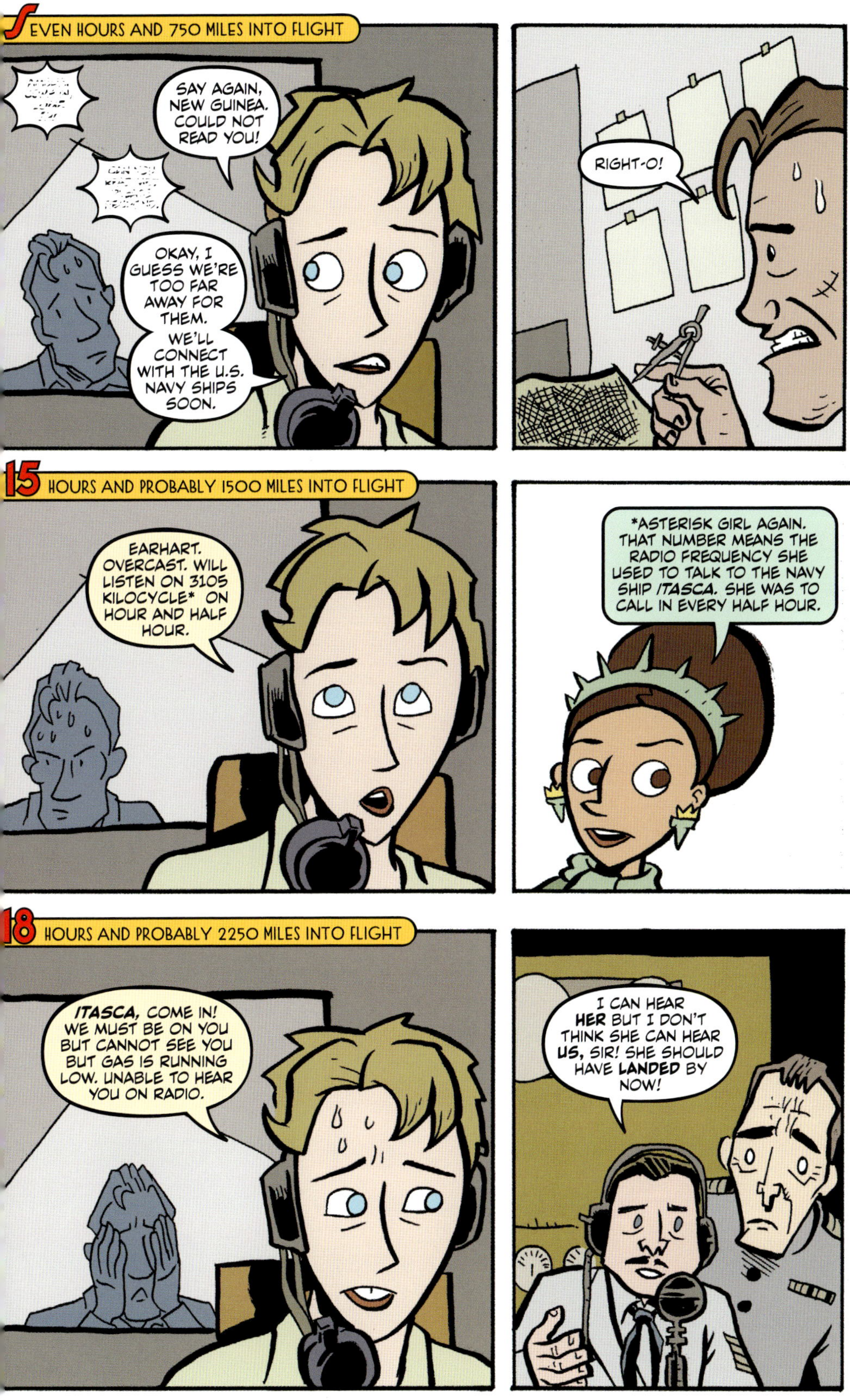
SEVEN HOURS AND 750 MILES INTO FLIGHT
SAY AGAIN, NEW GUINEA. COULD NOT READ YOU!
OKAY, I GUESS WE'RE TOO FAR AWAY FOR THEM.
WE'LL CONNECT WITH THE U.S. NAVY SHIPS SOON.
RIGHT-O!
15 HOURS AND PROBABLY 1500 MILES INTO FLIGHT
EARHART. OVERCAST. WILL LISTEN ON 3105 KILOCYCLE* ON HOUR AND HALF HOUR.
*ASTERISK GIRL AGAIN. THAT NUMBER MEANS THE RADIO FREQUENCY SHE USED TO TALK TO THE NAVY SHIP ITASCA. SHE WAS TO CALL IN EVERY HALF HOUR.
18 HOURS AND PROBABLY 2250 MILES INTO FLIGHT
ITASCA, COME IN! WE MUST BE ON YOU BUT CANNOT SEE YOU BUT GAS IS RUNNING LOW. UNABLE TO HEAR YOU ON RADIO.
I CAN HEAR HER BUT I DON'T THINK SHE CAN HEAR US, SIR! SHE SHOULD HAVE LANDED BY NOW!

7:42 AM (LOCAL TIME)

EARHART CALLING *ITASCA.* WE ARE CIRCLING BUT CANNOT HEAR YOU.

COME IN! COME IN! PLEASE REPEAT!

8:00 AM (LOCAL TIME)

WE RECEIVED YOUR SIGNALS BUT UNABLE TO GET A MINIMUM*. PLEASE TAKE BEARING ON US AND ANSWER ON 3105 WITH VOICE.

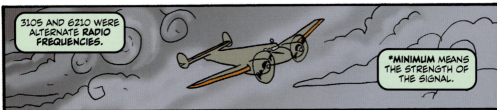

3105 AND 6210 WERE ALTERNATE **RADIO** FREQUENCIES.

*MINIMUM MEANS THE STRENGTH OF THE SIGNAL.

I CAN'T GET A **BEARING** ON HER, SIR. THE SIGNAL IS NOT **STRONG** ENOUGH!

8:43 AM (LOCAL TIME)

WE ARE ON LINE 157 337.

WILL REPEAT THIS MESSAGE ON 6210...

WE ARE RUNNING NORTH AND SOUTH.

NOTHING, SIR. I CAN'T HEAR A **THING**.

WHAT **HAPPENED?** WHERE DID THEY GO?

NO ONE KNOWS. THAT WAS THE LAST ANYONE **HEARD** FROM AMELIA EARHART.

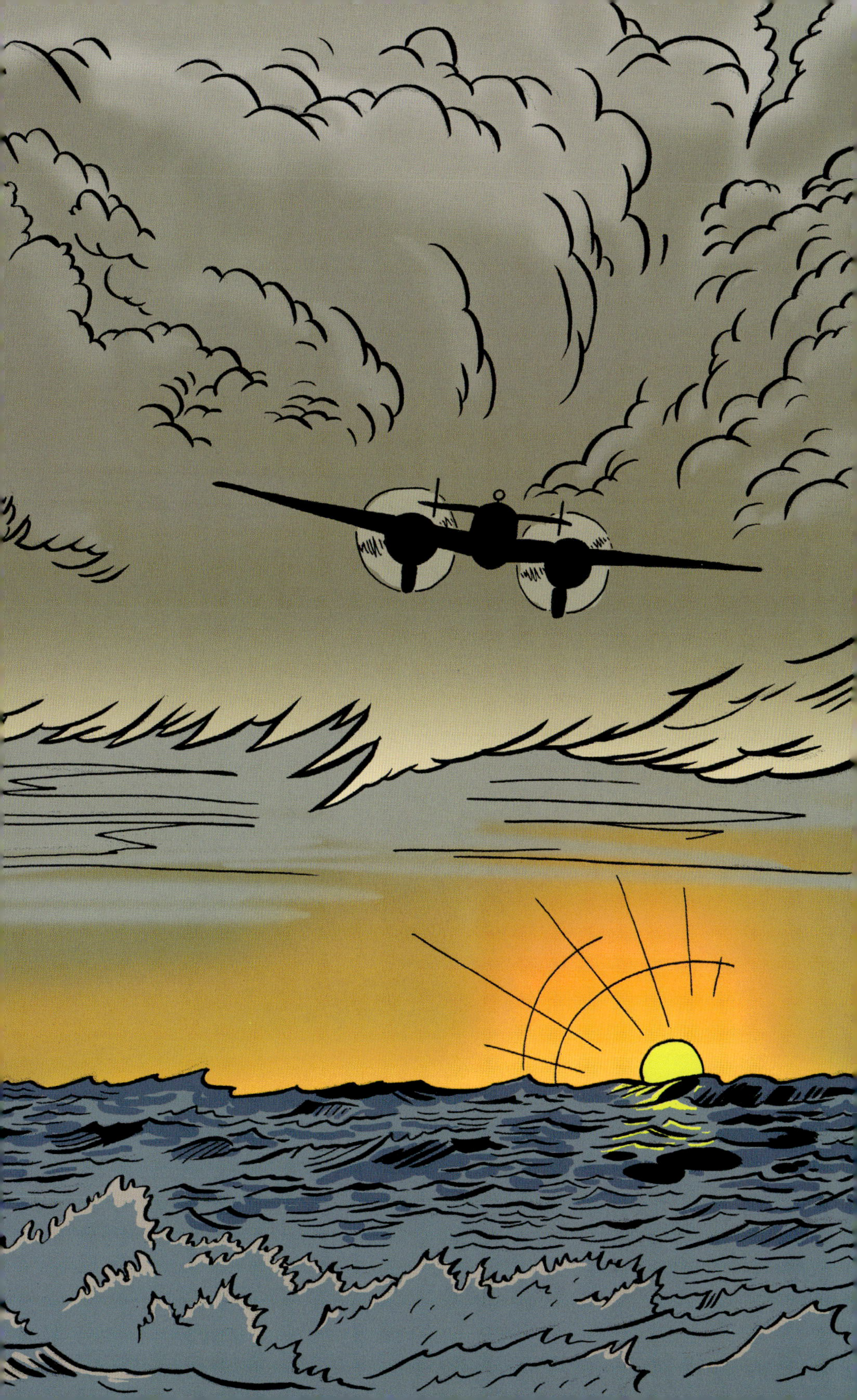

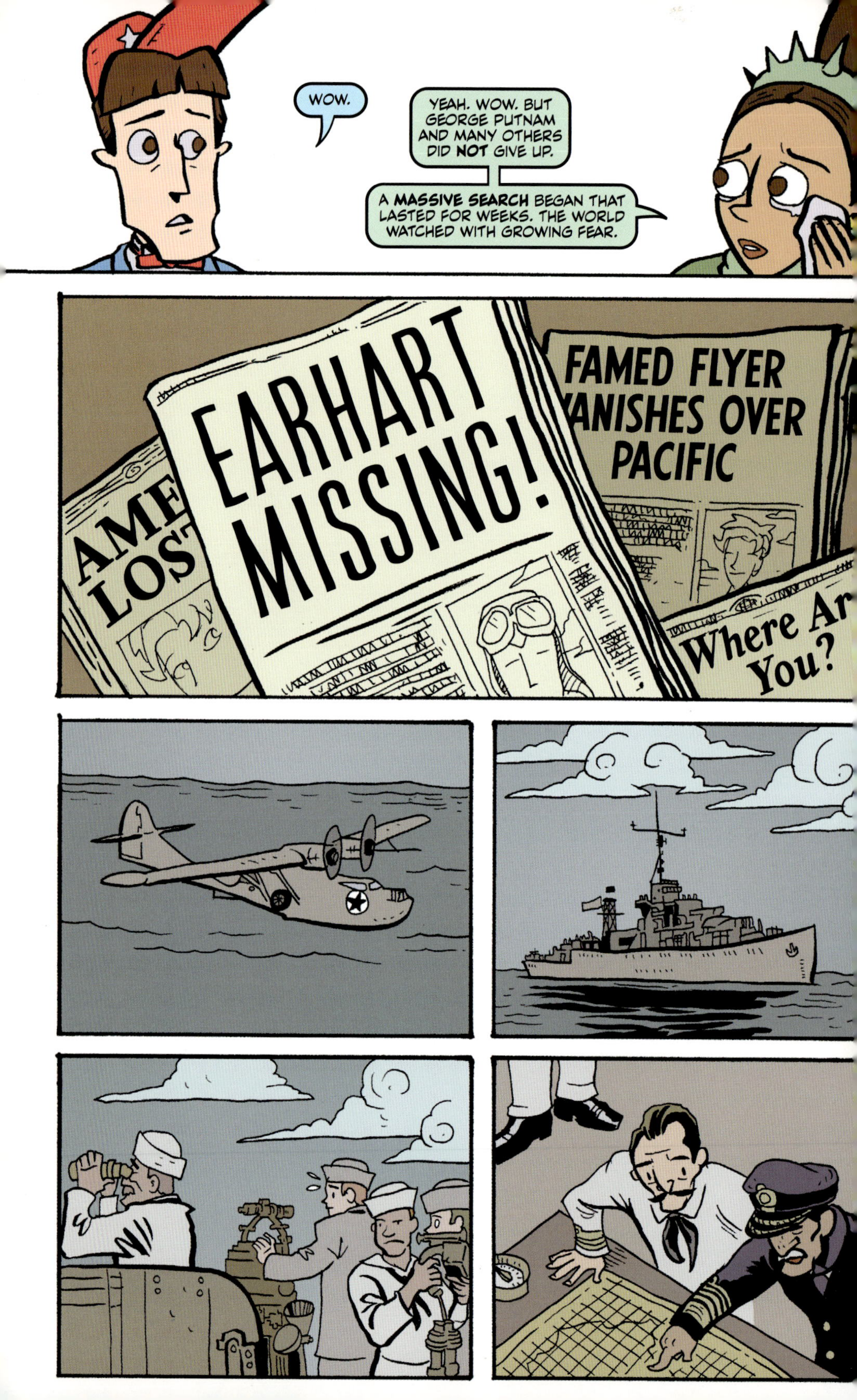
WOW.
YEAH. WOW. BUT GEORGE PUTNAM AND MANY OTHERS DID **NOT** GIVE UP.
A **MASSIVE SEARCH** BEGAN THAT LASTED FOR WEEKS. THE WORLD WATCHED WITH GROWING FEAR.
EARHART MISSING!
FAMED FLYER VANISHES OVER PACIFIC
Where Are You?

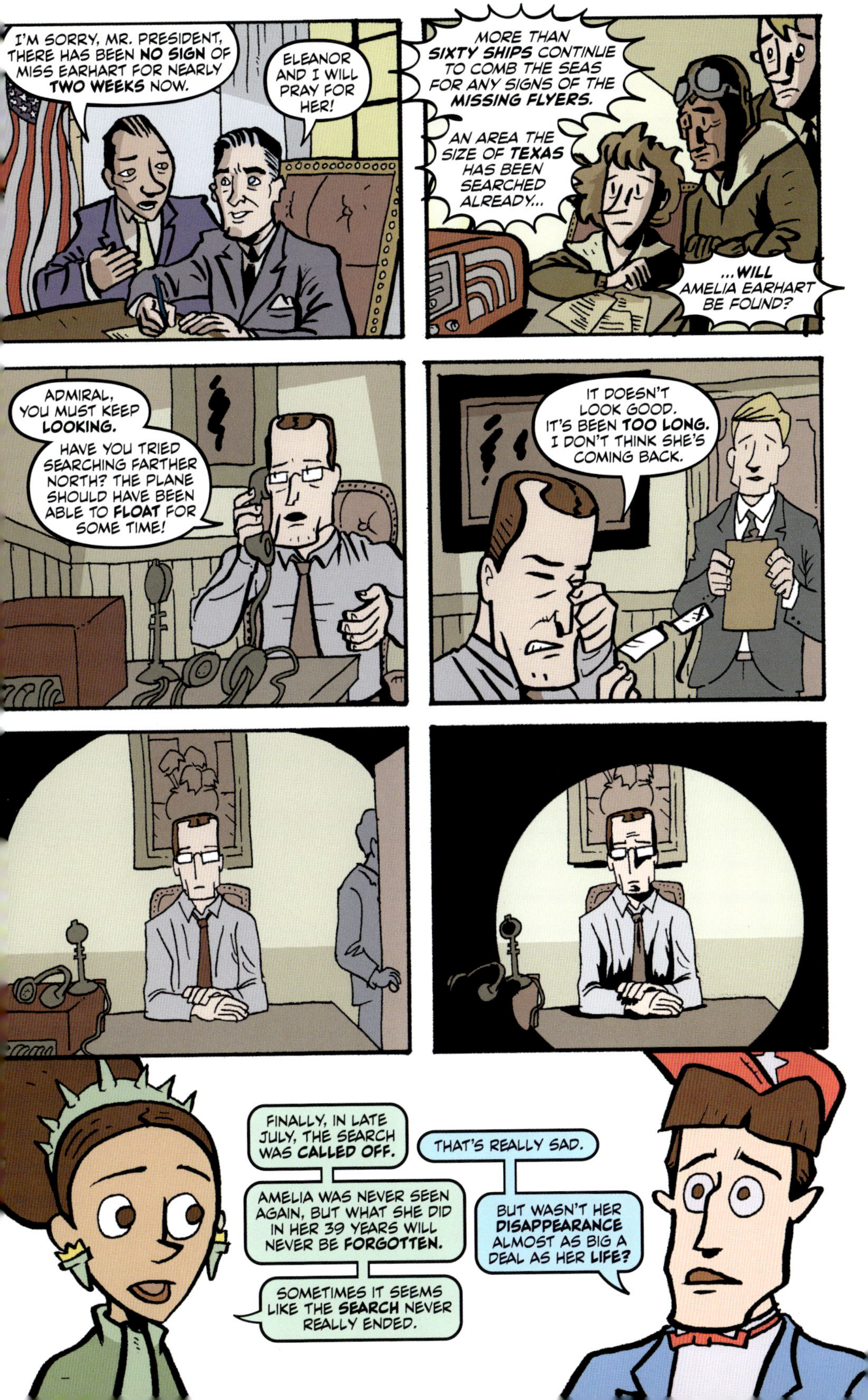
I'M SORRY, MR. PRESIDENT, THERE HAS BEEN **NO SIGN** OF MISS EARHART FOR NEARLY **TWO WEEKS** NOW.
ELEANOR AND I WILL PRAY FOR HER!
MORE THAN **SIXTY SHIPS** CONTINUE TO COMB THE SEAS FOR ANY SIGNS OF THE **MISSING FLYERS.**
AN AREA THE SIZE OF **TEXAS** HAS BEEN SEARCHED ALREADY...
...WILL AMELIA EARHART BE FOUND?
ADMIRAL, YOU MUST KEEP **LOOKING.**
HAVE YOU TRIED SEARCHING FARTHER NORTH? THE PLANE SHOULD HAVE BEEN ABLE TO **FLOAT** FOR SOME TIME!
IT DOESN'T LOOK GOOD. IT'S BEEN **TOO LONG.** I DON'T THINK SHE'S COMING BACK.
FINALLY, IN LATE JULY, THE SEARCH WAS **CALLED OFF.**
AMELIA WAS NEVER SEEN AGAIN, BUT WHAT SHE DID IN HER 39 YEARS WILL NEVER BE **FORGOTTEN.**
SOMETIMES IT SEEMS LIKE THE **SEARCH** NEVER REALLY ENDED.
THAT'S REALLY SAD.
BUT WASN'T HER **DISAPPEARANCE** ALMOST AS BIG A DEAL AS HER **LIFE?**

EXCLUSIVE! THE EARHART DISAPPEARANCE THEORIES.

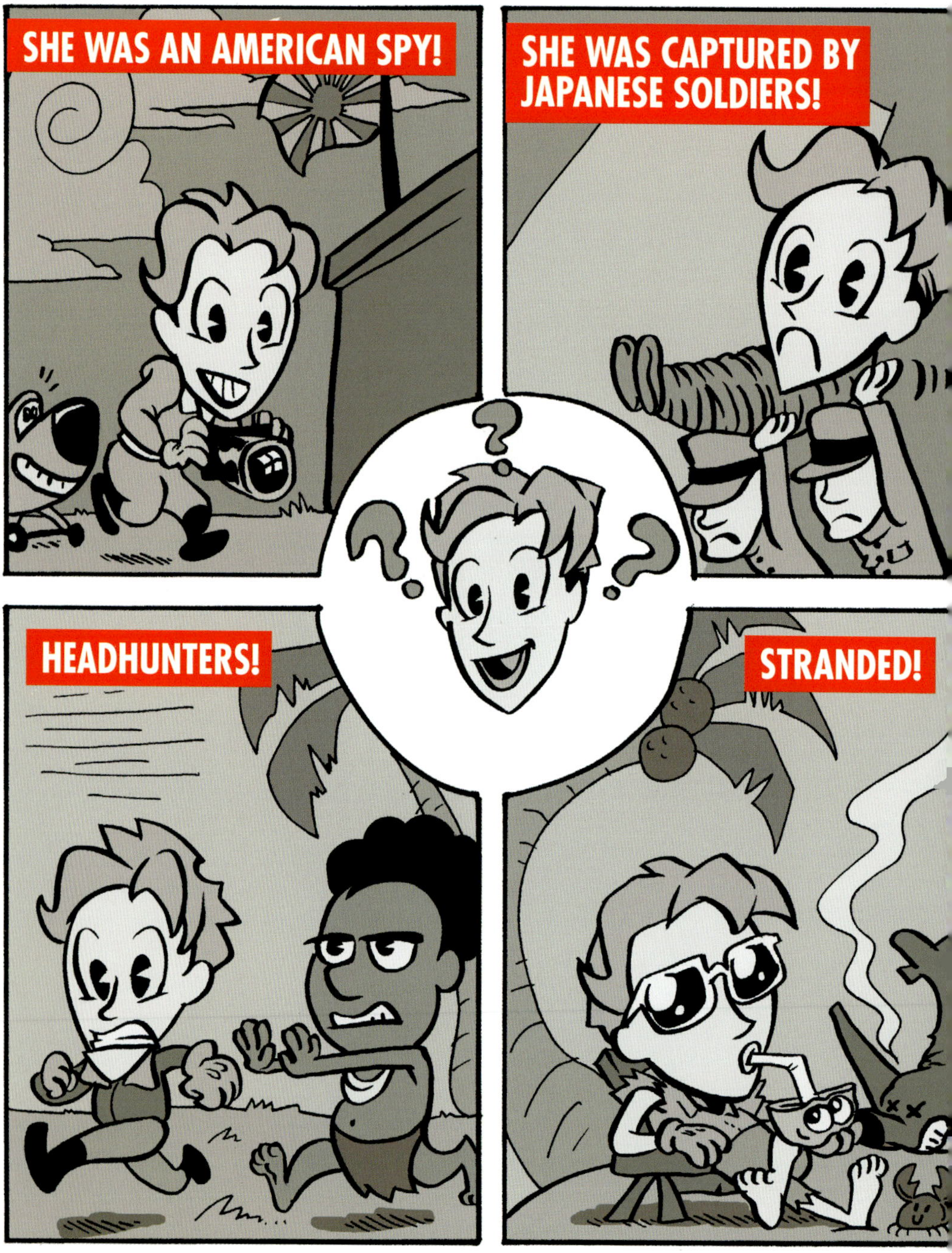

SHE WAS AN AMERICAN SPY!
SHE WAS CAPTURED BY JAPANESE SOLDIERS!
HEADHUNTERS!
STRANDED!

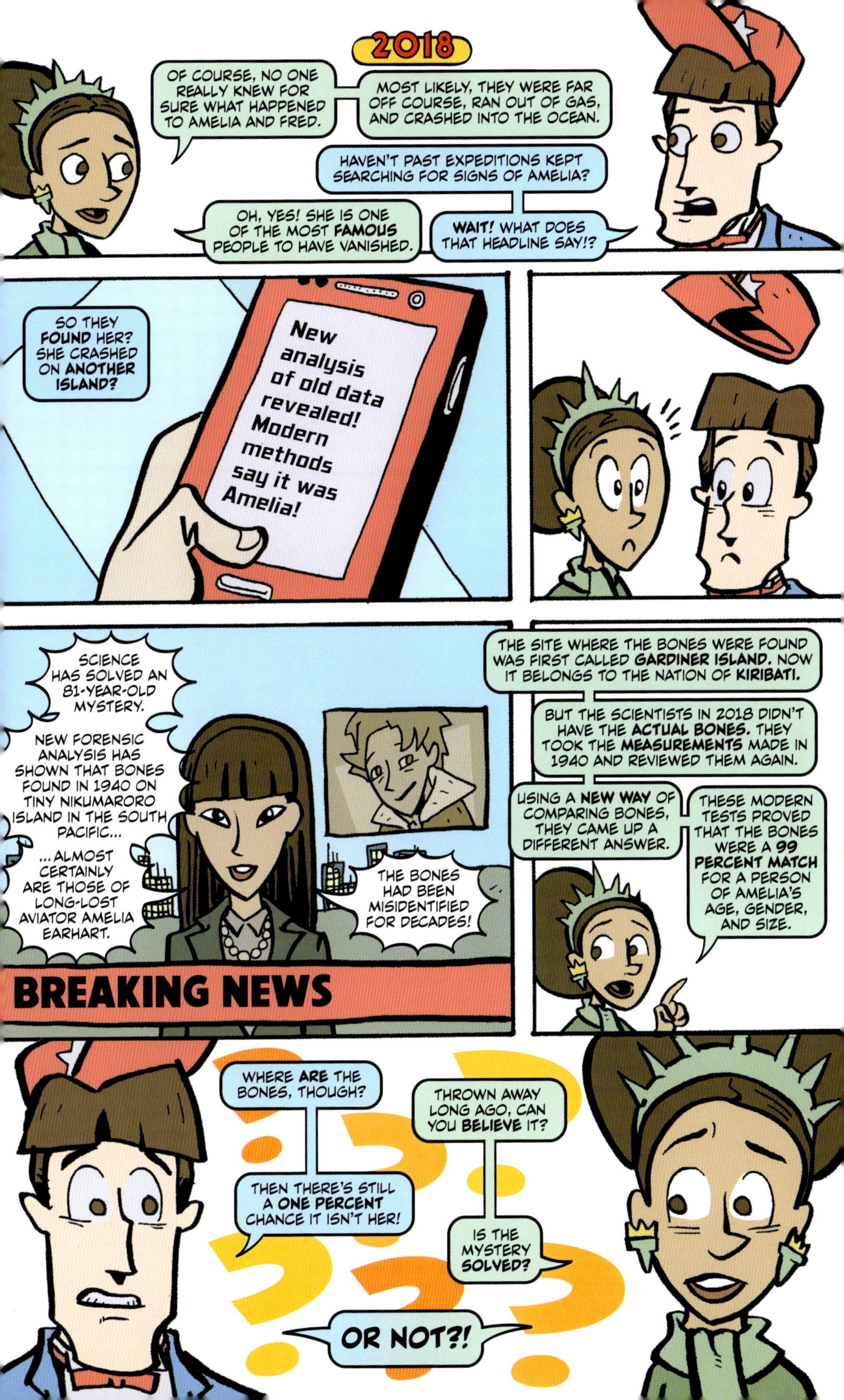

2018
OF COURSE, NO ONE REALLY KNEW FOR SURE WHAT HAPPENED TO AMELIA AND FRED.
MOST LIKELY, THEY WERE FAR OFF COURSE, RAN OUT OF GAS, AND CRASHED INTO THE OCEAN.
HAVEN'T PAST EXPEDITIONS KEPT SEARCHING FOR SIGNS OF AMELIA?
OH, YES! SHE IS ONE OF THE MOST FAMOUS PEOPLE TO HAVE VANISHED.
WAIT! WHAT DOES THAT HEADLINE SAY!?
SO THEY FOUND HER? SHE CRASHED ON ANOTHER ISLAND?
New analysis of old data revealed! Modern methods say it was Amelia!
SCIENCE HAS SOLVED AN 81-YEAR-OLD MYSTERY.
NEW FORENSIC ANALYSIS HAS SHOWN THAT BONES FOUND IN 1940 ON TINY NIKUMARORO ISLAND IN THE SOUTH PACIFIC...
...ALMOST CERTAINLY ARE THOSE OF LONG-LOST AVIATOR AMELIA EARHART.
THE BONES HAD BEEN MISIDENTIFIED FOR DECADES!
BREAKING NEWS
THE SITE WHERE THE BONES WERE FOUND WAS FIRST CALLED GARDINER ISLAND. NOW IT BELONGS TO THE NATION OF KIRIBATI.
BUT THE SCIENTISTS IN 2018 DIDN'T HAVE THE ACTUAL BONES. THEY TOOK THE MEASUREMENTS MADE IN 1940 AND REVIEWED THEM AGAIN.
USING A NEW WAY OF COMPARING BONES, THEY CAME UP A DIFFERENT ANSWER.
THESE MODERN TESTS PROVED THAT THE BONES WERE A 99 PERCENT MATCH FOR A PERSON OF AMELIA'S AGE, GENDER, AND SIZE.
WHERE ARE THE BONES, THOUGH?
THROWN AWAY LONG AGO, CAN YOU BELIEVE IT?
THEN THERE'S STILL A ONE PERCENT CHANCE IT ISN'T HER!
IS THE MYSTERY SOLVED?
OR NOT?!

FAMOUS FLYING WOMEN!

HARRIET QUIMBY was the first woman in America to earn her pilot's license. In 1912, she gained world attention by flying along across the English Channel. Sadly, Quimby died later the same year in a crash.

In 1921, **BESSIE COLEMAN** became the first woman to earn an international pilot's license. She was also the first African American to obtain a license. She, too, died tragically in a crash in 1926.

JACQUELINE COCHRAN was the most accomplished female pilot of the first half of the 20th century. She won the Harmon Trophy as top pilot 14 times and was the first woman to land and take off from an aircraft carrier. She also trained female pilots during World War II.

In 1964, **JERRIE MOCK** became the first woman to complete Earhart's quest by successfully flying around the world. She did the job in 29 days.

EMILY WARNER was the first woman hired as a pilot by a commercial airline. In 1973, she took the controls for Frontier Airlines.

VICTORIA VAN METER flew across the United States in 1993. What was the big deal? Well, she was only 11! She had a copilot, but Victoria did all the work!

AMELIA EARHART WAS NOT THE **ONLY** RECORD-BREAKING FEMALE PILOT. DO SOME RESEARCH TO FIND OUT MORE ABOUT **THESE** PIONEERS!

AMELIA EARHART TIMELINE

1897 Amelia is born on July 24 in Kansas.

1916 She graduates from high school after moving to Chicago.

1917 With her sister, Amelia begins work as a nurse in a Toronto military hospital.

1921 Amelia moves to Los Angeles, begins taking flying lessons.

1925 Amelia works at a settlement house in Boston.

1928 With two other pilots, she becomes the first woman to fly across the Atlantic Ocean. Later, she becomes the first woman to fly across the United States (making several stops along the way).

1931 Amelia marries publisher and publicist George Putnam.

1932 On May 21, Amelia becomes the first woman to fly solo across the Atlantic.

1935 Amelia goes on a national speaking tour, and then is the first person to fly nonstop from Hawaii to California. Later in the year, she becomes the first woman to complete a flight from Mexico City to New Jersey.

1937 On June 1, Amelia begins her flight around the world with navigator Fred Noonan. On July 2, radio contact with the pair is lost while they fly from New Guinea across the Pacific Ocean.

GLOSSARY

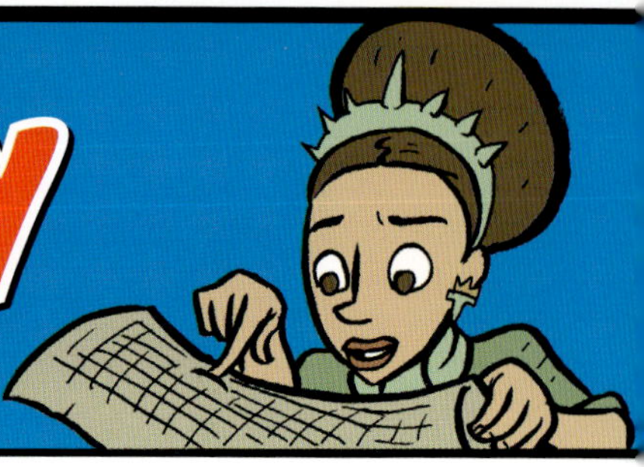

"ACROSS THE POND": Slang for crossing the Atlantic Ocean between Europe and America.

ALTIMETER: A device in an airplane that measures altitude.

ALTITUDE: Height above a surface, like land or sea level.

AUTOGYRO: An experimental aircraft that had a propellor on top like a helicopter, and wings like an airplane.

AVIATOR: The pilot or operator of an airplane.

BEARING: A direction something is coming from or moving along.

FREQUENCY: In radio, the wavelength that is like an "address" for people using the radio.

HANGARS: Large buildings that house airplanes.

KILOCYCLE: A measurement of radio waves.

MECHANIZED: Run by a machine.

PERIL: Danger.

PERSISTED: Kept going, no matter what.

SETTLEMENT HOUSE: Buildings that housed and helped poor people.

TRICE: Old-time term for "in a hurry."

WORLD WAR I: Conflict among countries in Europe that lasted from 1914-1918.

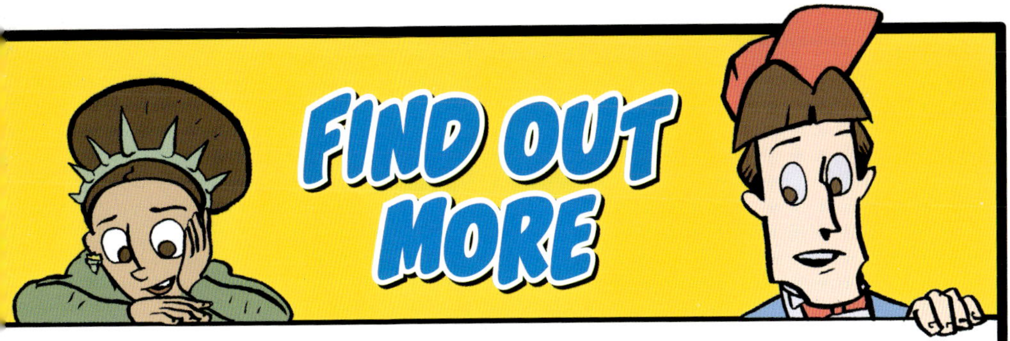

FIND OUT MORE

BOOKS

Fleming, Candace. *Amelia Lost: The Life and Disappearance of Amelia Earhart*. Boston: Schwartz & Wade, 2011.

Harmon, Daniel. *Aviation Pioneer*. Britannica Beginner Bios series. New York: Britannica Educational Publishing, 2018.

Jerome, Kate Boehm. *Who Was Amelia Earhart?* Who Was? series. New York: Penguin Group, 2002.

Lovell, Mary S. *The Sound of Wings: The Life of Amelia Earhart*. New York: St. Martin's Press, 1989.

Rich, Doris L. *Amelia Earhart: A Biography*. Washington, DC: Smithsonian Institution, 1989.

Stone, Tanya Lee. *Amelia Earhart*. DK Biography series. New York: DK Books, 2007.

WEBSITES

Biography: Amelia Earhart (including short video)
https://www.biography.com/people/amelia-earhart-9283280

Biography.com
A documentary about Amelia.
https://www.biography.com/video/amelia-earhart-full-episode-2071933358

Library of Congress, The
America's Story from America's Library: Amelia Earhart
http://www.americaslibrary.gov/aa/earhart/aa_earhart_subj.html

Ninety-Nines International Organization of Women Pilots
https://www.ninety-nines.org

VIDEO

Amelia Earhart: The Price of Courage. American Experience series. Washington, DC: PBS, 1993.

SHOW ME HISTORY!

COLLECT EVERY BOOK IN THE SERIES AND FIND THE *STORY* IN HISTORY!

SHOW ME HISTORY!
ALEXANDER HAMILTON
The FIGHTING FOUNDING FATHER!
MARK SHULMAN • KELLY TINDALL

SHOW ME HISTORY!
MARTIN LUTHER KING Jr.
VOICE for EQUALITY!
JAMES BUCKLEY JR. • YOUNEEK STUDIOS

SHOW ME HISTORY!
ABRAHAM LINCOLN
DEFENDER of the UNION!
MARK SHULMAN • TOM MARTIN

PARENTS AND TEACHERS: VISIT OUR WEBSITE FOR MORE *SHOW ME HISTORY!* FUN:

WWW.SHOWMEHISTORY.COM

Enjoy a video about the series.

Learn more about the authors and illustrators.

Download a free preview of each book.

Sign up for our email newsletter.

Access our *Show Me History! Reading Guide*, perfect for teachers, librarians, homeschoolers, and parents.

FOLLOW US ON SOCIAL MEDIA:

www.facebook.com/portablepress

www.pinterest.com/portablepress

@portablepress

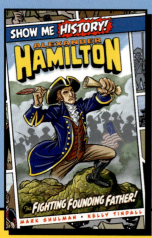

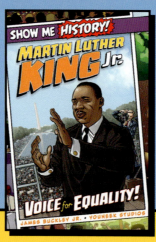

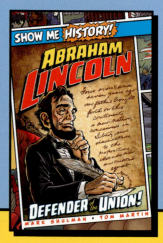